WINNING STRATEGIES FOR MANAGING PEOPLE

WINNING STRATEGIES FOR MANAGING PEOPLE

A Task Directed Guide

ROBERT IRWIN and **RITA WOLENIK**

Kogan
Page

This book is a text on managing employees in the workplace. It does not aim to be a guide to current employment law, for which managers should refer to the latest personnel manuals.

First published in the United States of America
in 1985 by Franklin Watts, New York

Copyright © Robert Irwin and Rita Wolenik 1985

This edition first published in Great Britain
in 1986 by Kogan Page Ltd, 120 Pentonville Road,
London N1 9JN

Additional material copyright © Kogan Page 1986

All rights reserved

British Library Cataloguing in Publication Data
Irwin, Robert, *1941-*
    Winning strategies for managing people :
    a task directed guide.
    1. Personnel management
    I. Title   II. Wolenik, Rita
    658.3   HF5549

    ISBN 1-85091-192-4
    ISBN 1-85091-193-2 Pbk

Printed and bound in Great Britain by
Billing & Sons Limited, Worcester

A typical procedure 103; Documentation 104; Time-scale 106; Pitfalls to avoid 106

Preface

The most successful manager is not the one who does the job fastest. The most successful manager is the one who does the best job.

Yet 'lack of time' is the most common complaint heard from managers. As managers, we are constantly looking for ways to go faster. 'Look at all the time we'd save', we think, if we could do everything in five-minute or even one-minute spurts of energy.

The trouble is that addressing time directly doesn't really solve much in the real world. *Lack of time isn't the problem.* It's the symptom. Good managers will have plenty of time because of their successful techniques. Poor managers will never have enough no matter how fast they try to go.

Can you imagine the managers at NASA more than a decade ago saying, 'What we need is a space shuttle. Now I want each person to take one minute to come up with a way to do it!'

Being quick wasn't nearly as important as being right. The *true* test for the shuttle, after all, was not how fast it was developed, but that it flew.

To build a space shuttle or to hire, fire, and build a good employee involves knowledge of where you're going and understanding of how to get there.

This book gives you both. We shall look at the strategies that you as a manager must have in order to manage successfully. More important, we'll break these down into 15 specific tasks. Each task is really a discrete strategy that you can use to get the specific management result you want. It's important to understand that you can use any of the strategy tasks in this book at any time. You don't have to start at the beginning and work your way through each task in order. If you need to dismiss someone, look up the tasks on dismissal. If you need to criticise a worker, see the task labelled criticism. If you need to conduct a job interview, see the task on interviewing. You will get instant information on how to solve your immediate problem.

This book is designed to make your job as a manager easier, not to burden you with more things to do. This book will not cost you time, it will save you time.

Once you start using the strategy task approach, you'll find that you are able to move quickly and easily through what otherwise could be difficult, emotion-charged situations. You will suddenly find you have much more time available for accomplishing other tasks.

The goal of this book is to address the source, not the symptom. Its aim is to give you the right answer, when you need it, for the problem you have right now.

The Tasks

Task 1

Recruitment Objectives

We've never met a job applicant who didn't want to be successful, but that doesn't mean that every applicant is going to be a success. Many are simply the wrong person for the job. The cost of appointing the wrong person can be high. A mistake will reflect badly on you. What's worse, you may end up carrying the person and doing his or her job as well as your own. And ultimately, you may not be able to achieve your own work goals because you don't have the support from below.

As a manager, your goal is to appoint only the right person. You want to do this with a minimum amount of time, energy and emotional stress. You don't want to spend weeks finding a new employee; that would take too much time away from your own important work. Think of all the energy and time you'd have available to spend on the other important aspects of your job if the next time you need to take someone on you could accomplish the task without fear or anxiety and could do it with great certainty of getting the right person.

The goal of this chapter is to show you how to determine the right person for the job – quickly and easily.

How do you find the right person?

We once knew a manager who had a quick personnel method. He took on the first person who responded to his job advertisement regardless of who that person was. He swore that it didn't matter, that he could take anyone – anyone at all – and with six months of training have that person successfully doing any job!

There's probably a lot more truth to that conviction than

most managers would care to admit! And it's unlikely that many would put it into practice. The risk of getting the wrong person is too great: most people are going to do everything possible to get just the right person for the job.

But exactly how is that done? Most managers don't have a *person strategy*. So they come up with an often ill-conceived plan thought up on the spur of the moment.

A spur-of-the-moment plan

Has this ever happened to you? Suddenly you need to recruit someone. Your first thoughts are these:

1. With all the work I have to do, now I have the job of recruiting someone on top of it. (Dislike)
2. If I don't get the right person for the job, the result will reflect on my abilities as a manager. (Fear)
3. I'll have to get started right away. I'll need to write a job description and put an ad in the paper, then I'll need to read CVs and then I'll have to interview. My God, how will I get everything done? (Scrambling)

Most managers improvise a plan each time they need to recruit. That, however, is not the best way – or even a satisfactory way – of doing it. The results can be most dissatisfying. You can end up with a person who really wants to do something else, who took your job to fill in until the right job comes along. Perhaps your new employee really wants to be a singer. She gives you only part-time energy and part-time dedication while working full-time towards her chosen career.

Or perhaps your new worker really wants to be out in the field selling or interviewing, but he's taken a desk job because he needed work right away and that's all that was available. He may try to do good work, but with his heart outside, he isn't going to be able to produce the kind of enthusiasm and energy you may demand.

Getting the right person

To get the right person for the job, you need to know exactly what the person's own goals are. You need to know that the person is operating on the same wave-length as you are, and really wants to do the work the job offers. This means not only having a job description (which we'll get to in the next chapter) but also a 'person description'. This is both easier and harder than it sounds. It's easier because creating a person description is fairly simple. It's harder because most people tend to forget to use such a description even when they have it.

Therefore, to begin, you need to have a 'person objectives' strategy. You set down your goals for the person you need. You put the paper aside and have it ready. Whenever you need to take someone on, you whip out your goals and modify them, if necessary, to the particular job. There's no worry, no fear, and no wasted time. You don't need to scramble. You just look at your objectives and find the person who fits.

Defining your 'person objectives'

Each time you appoint staff, you must remember that it is part of a long-term process. The danger is that you will consider only your goals of the moment: you need someone right now who's willing to do the work at the salary offered and is pleasant to be around.

You must realise that recruiting isn't just a single, unrelated incident in your work day. It is part of a process that involves the entire term of employment. It's a process that involves a *long-term* relationship.

Your objective is success six months, a year, three years, five years, or longer down the road. You're planning for the future as well as for the present.

Once you remember you're involved in a long-term process, you can define your long- and short-term objectives for the person you want.

Person description

Short-term objectives typically are such things as:

1. Someone who'll take the job right away.
2. Someone with at least minimum experience.
3. Someone who can communicate with me.

You undoubtedly have your own short-term objectives to add to this list.

15

Long-term objectives, on the other hand, are quite different. The employee may not be able to achieve these today. The question is, will he or she be able to achieve them during the full course of employment?

Typical long-term employee objectives are:

1. *Results.* The employee will work on a specific project and complete it satisfactorily in a specific time.
2. *Independence.* The employee will be able to work (a) independently (b) with little supervision (c) with moderate supervision.
3. *Work habits.* The employee will cooperate and work as part of a team.
4. *Dedication.* The employee will demonstrate dedication by applying to the job discipline, creativity, and whatever talents he or she may have. The employee will also give 'quality time' and energy to the job.
5. *Motivation.* The employee will be enthusiastic, ready to meet the job's challenge.
6. *Loyalty.* The employee will support me, the company, and the project.

Your objectives may be different (but probably not much different) from these, and you may have additional ones. It's important to remember, however, that you need to define your goals for the person you eventually take on. If you don't first set objectives for the person you're looking for, how will you recognise your new employee when you see him or her?

Hint. All of these objectives are really specific ways of stating the general objective that the employee will make a strong commitment to the job. It doesn't matter whether the employee is going to be selling fried chicken at a fast-food take-away or making million-pound loans at a bank. During the time the employee is working for you, what you want is commitment to the job. The trick, of course, is to identify commitment.

The building blocks of recruitment

Once you know what your goals for the person are, how do you determine whether or not an applicant fits them?

Recruitment is not a single act. It requires making a series of decisions, each depending on the next. There is a job description to write, applicants to be sought, CVs to read, and interviews to conduct. You've done the first, but important, step: you've determined who you are looking for. The rest of it is trying to find that person.

Finding the right person, even if you know what you want, can still seem overwhelming if you try to tackle the whole thing at once. It's like trying to eat a whole pie; your stomach would surely balk. However, if you cut it up into smaller slices and then eat each slice separately over a period of time, not only will you finish the pie, but you'll enjoy it, too!

The next chapters cover each of the tasks involved and show you how to accomplish them quickly and easily.

The first step, however, is knowing who you are looking for. Once you have your 'person objectives' in hand, you'll feel much more comfortable about making the decisions.

Recruitment and Job Descriptions

In order to attract applicants you must be able to describe the job you are offering. We'll first cover writing the job description, then using it to recruit.

Writing the job description

Written job descriptions are used for classified ads, vacancy boards, employment agencies, in fact for almost any source you have, including the applicants themselves. People who are looking for jobs need to know what you are offering. You tell them in the job description. That's why they are so important. They are not hard to write and can be done in a matter of a few minutes. Before we go into the technique of writing them, there are two areas to consider:

1. Remember that this is a *job* description, not an applicant description. Applicant descriptions are something you keep in mind as you go through the recruiting steps (see Task 1). The goal here is to get an applicant who is qualified for the *job*. By the time you begin interviewing, every applicant you see should minimally qualify for the position you're trying to fill.
2. The job description should avoid any hint of discrimination. That means it must not discriminate against any person because of their race or sex.

The actual description

Always think of a job description as having *two* parts. In the first part, you describe what the employee will do *on the job*. In the second part, you describe the qualifications the employee must have for doing it. The easiest way to accomplish this is to draw a line down the middle of the page. On the left side indicate what the employee will do. On the right, list the qualification for doing it.

For example, if you are looking for someone to deliver express packages, the left side of the sheet will read:

Will handle
delivery route

Now put the requirement for handling a delivery route on the right side:

Must have
a commercial
driver's licence

You start on the left and just describe what the person will do in the job. Then you work out what the requirement for that might be. Everything that a person does on the job has some sort of requirement. For example, perhaps you're looking for a copy editor for a house journal. The sheet might read:

Will write	*Must have a BA*
and edit copy	*degree in English*
	and be able to
	spell accurately

Or you might be hiring a cashier:

Will work on	*Must be bondable*
cash register in	
retail outlet	

Or maybe you need a salesperson:

Will handle	*Must have prior*
over-the-counter	*sales experience*
sales of	*in field*
feminine products	*with feminine*
	merchandise

When you've listed a complete description of what the person will do 'on the job' on the left side and a complete set of requirements 'for the job' on the right side, simply put together all the items on the left side as a first paragraph and all the items on the right side as a second paragraph and you have a comprehensive, detailed, and accurate job description ready to use.

Hint. Items that are done 'on the job' usually start with 'will'. The applicant *will* do this or that. Items that are requirements usually start with 'must'. Applicant *must* have this or that.

Recruiting

Recruiting is so important it should not be left to anyone but yourself. If you have a personnel department, however, the manager there will cover the first stages for you, leaving you to choose from the short list.

Remember, the employee you finally hire will come from the pool of applicants you use. There are many sources of applicants. They are listed here in terms of those we have found to be most promising to least promising.

Sources of applicants

1. *Referrals* from other people you know in the business. Posting on notice boards within the company can also be a source here. Some companies pay a bonus to employees for successful referrals.
2. *Re-engaging* former employees with proven records. Some companies keep track of former employees for just this purpose.
3. *Promotion* from inside the company, as long as you provide proper training. (It's important not to get trapped into promoting just on the basis of seniority; you could end up with the wrong person for the job.)
4. *The milk round.* Offers are made in advance of graduation dependent on results. A tour of selected universities is involved to recruit future high flyers.
5. *Classified advertising* in papers and trade journals likely to be read by potential employees.
6. *Stealing* by using 'head hunters' to lure staff from your competitors. (This is very costly and there is the danger that the person you take on may be the person your competitor was just getting ready to drop.)
7. *Management consultants* are a good choice when top

managers, directors or high-level technicians are required.

8. *Employment agencies* can be a good source for lower-paying jobs if you get to know someone you can trust in the agency. Otherwise they tend not to vet applicants too carefully.

9. *Careers offices and careers teachers in schools and colleges.* Depending on the job both these sources will provide applicants.

10. *Jobcentres.* The applicants here sometimes really don't want the particular job but apply because there's little or no choice.

11. *Application file.* You call up personnel and ask, 'Who do we have on file for such-and-such a job.' You may get an indiscriminate list of on-spec applicants as a response.

To find the *top* applicants you may need to start at the beginning of the list and work through to the end. A lot depends on luck, on the time you have available, and on the contacts you've established.

Screening the CVs and Job Applications

Many managers complain that they just don't have time to read through CVs and/or job application forms. That's probably because they don't know what they are reading them for. You can read a large stack of these in 30 minutes or less, *if* you know what to look for.

It's important to understand that CVs and/or applications are more negative than positive. While it's true that you normally look for something in them that will make you want to interview the applicant, it's more likely that you are looking for something that will allow you to *eliminate* the person. Typically, you may have several dozen applicants, but you want to conduct only half a dozen interviews or less. The CV and/or application thus becomes a device for separating the chaff from the wheat. It lets you cull those who you think can't handle the job.

If that's the case, then you must be very good at your reading. If you're careless, or if you delegate the reading to others, you just might find yourself throwing out the very best candidates and interviewing the less desirable ones.

Pop-ups

When reading CVs and/or applications there are certain items to watch out for. We call these 'pop-ups' because they often pop up out of the background of what's written.

If you know what these pop-ups are, you can scan a CV and/or application for them quickly and in just a few moments make a decision on whether or not to interview.

Pop-up 1: Direction

Read the part of the CV that shows previous work experience over the past 10 years. Has the applicant been moving towards the kind of work you have to offer? Or has the movement been in the other direction? You don't want to hire someone whose mind lies elsewhere.

Another item to look for is 'stature'. Has the person's previous work experience been appropriate to the stature of the job you offer? (If it has been higher, the applicant may feel this job is a step down.)

Finally, look for 'achievements'. In this world there are 'doers' and there are 'doddlers'. Does the applicant list any awards, prizes, or recognitions of accomplishments to show that they know how to get things done?

Pop-up 2: Multiples

The single best indicator of how the applicant will perform working for you is how he or she performed working for someone else. Look at work history. If the applicant has had a strong work history, there's every reason to think he or she will continue to be a strong worker.

The question, of course, is how do you know from the application? One good way is to check for 'multiples'. Multiples means that the applicant has either had multiple jobs over his or her work history *or* has had multiple duties within jobs. The best candidates usually have had *both*.

You can check multiple jobs by counting the *number* of past employers that the applicant has had. Many seasoned personnel people feel that the ideal candidate will have changed companies every three to four years. More often than that can mean a problem either in getting along with others or in work performance. Longer than five years in a job can mean the applicant is too set in his or her ways to adapt easily to new company demands.

Multiple *duties* are revealed by what the applicant has written with regard to 'responsibilities' or 'duties' on past jobs. (Every CV should include this information.) Look for an applicant who has had many different duties and responsibilities. The *variety* indicates competence, the ability to learn and, most important, that others have trusted the individual to move to increasing responsibilities.

This technique can be difficult to apply to younger applicants, particularly those just out of school. Nevertheless, you can look for multiples in school performance; extracurricular activities, outside interests, part-time jobs all indicate a positive and highly motivated person.

Pop-up 3: Salary progression

A person who has multiples should also show a steady upward movement in salary. In business, the rewards of good work are monetary. The pop-up here is when the applicant *fails to show or leaves out* salary progression. If he or she has not had a reasonable increase in salary over the years, then there is usually a good reason why the rewards of hard work have been denied.

Pop-up 4: Date gaps

A good CV should give work history from the time the applicant left school or at least for the past 10 years. In a normal CV this means *every bit of time*. If there is a gap between one job and the next, it is important to know why.

It can be for reasons as innocuous as taking a course or staying at home to raise children. Or it could be that the applicant was unemployable during that period. Was he or she in gaol? In a mental institution? Fighting bankruptcy proceedings?

Good applicants will usually make sure that every bit of their time is accounted for. They don't want you to think the worst.

Pop-up 5: Ambiguities

There's an old saying that goes, 'If you can't dazzle them with brilliance, baffle them with bullshit'. An applicant who has had successful job experiences should have no trouble clearly stating them. On the other hand, an applicant who wants to hide a bad job history or a problem may rely on ambiguities. In describing 'responsibilities' in a previous job, the applicant writes, 'In charge of multiple office operations'. Really? Does that mean he or she made coffee as well as running the post room?

Applicants who have something to hide and who do not lie,

will often use ambiguities on the theory that it's up to the employer to figure out what's meant. If the CV is ambiguous, a good rule of thumb is to assume there's a problem.

Another place this often occurs is when the application form asks, 'Reason for leaving job'; the applicant may write 'better job offer'. Indeed? Does the next job the applicant lists show increased responsibilities or higher salary? If not, how was it a better job offer? Remember, an ambiguous answer often is a cover-up for a problem.

Follow-up: Lying

These are items to check after you've selected those CVs/applications of applicants you think you might want to interview.

There are no degrees to lying. Either something is the truth or it's a lie. One lie on an application form should be enough to sink the applicant. (If the person lies on the application, what will they do on the job?)

Typical places for spotting lies are *starting and ending salaries*. The applicant knows exactly what salary he or she started and ended at or can quickly find out. Exaggerated claims here are just lies. These *sometimes* can be verified through reference checks. If you take the applicant on, their tax form P45 shows the pay received in the current tax year – too late maybe if their claims were exaggerated, but a discrepancy would make you keep an eye on them.

Another place where applicants sometimes lie is explaining why they left a company. An applicant may give one reason, but a simple check may reveal a bankruptcy or other problem.

Yet another area for lying has to do with education. Applicants may exaggerate qualifications or degrees. A letter to the registrar's office of the college, university or professional institution can be very revealing.

Reading a CV is really a job of elimination. If you know the pop-ups to look for, you can usually eliminate very quickly those applicants who aren't right for the job.

Task 4

Getting Honest Answers from References

Taking up references

If you're recruiting and you want honest references, how do you get them in an age of deception?

The answer is that you have to have a few tricks of your own.

When checking references be sure first to get permission from the applicant to contact those listed as referees.

Rule 1: Never say you're checking a reference

If you phone and say straight away that you're checking a reference, any alert employer or manager will immediately be on guard. He or she will know better than to say anything derogatory; perhaps they will not be willing to say anything at all. Thus if you call saying you're conducting a reference check, the answer probably is already 'No!'

Therefore, if you can't get information the direct way by saying you're checking a reference, you have to do it indirectly. Always begin by asking for the applicant's old boss (direct superior).

When you phone, say you only want to know if the applicant used to work there. A phrase such as 'verifying former employment' usually works well. Chances are even the most taciturn manager or employer will be willing to answer such an innocuous question.

A written application may be necessary for the personnel department. Enclose a stamped and addressed envelope so the reply comes directly to you. If you want to discuss the applicant, you can ring the personnel officer named as the signatory, who may well be willing to give extra information now that personal contact (and your bona fides) has been established. If there were problems with the employee, he or she may be willing to speak off the record.

Rule 2: Establish rapport

If you get an affirmative answer to your first question, try to strike up a conversation with the former boss. What product is made or service offered by the company? What is its correct address? Just ask simple questions that you could find out from the telephone book. Don't hint that what the former boss says will influence a decision on whether to engage the applicant.

If the former boss seems to want to talk, yet is hesitant, don't assume it's the questions you're asking. You don't know who may be within earshot of the conversation at the other end. Maybe he or she feels uncomfortable discussing the former employee at that moment. Ask if you can call back later, or on a different number (his direct line).

Rule 3: Never ask leading questions

Don't ask the former boss to give you his or her impression of the employee. Don't ask if the employee had any problems. Don't ask about weaknesses. These will immediately put the former boss on guard. Remember, he or she can simply hang up on you at any time.

Instead ask if the former boss will *verify* what the applicant has already told you. The boss only has to answer 'yes' or 'no' to questions about what the former employee did, not their performance. Now read off the description given by the applicant of his or her former job. (You may want especially to consider duties that you think the applicant will need to perform on the current job.) Sniggers or long pauses here can tell you a lot.

Finally, if you've established good rapport, the former boss may volunteer some insights into the past employee. If the boss mentions that the employee was 'particularly good' at this or that, it could mean that the applicant was 'not particularly good' at things not praised.

Using other sources

The 'old boy' network

Another very productive fount of information on applicants can be your own contacts. If you're an engineer from Imperial College or Cranfield, for example, and you have an applicant from a company which might itself have an engineer from your college, you might give your old college 'chum' a call. Even if you've never met the person, the fact that you went to the same college can sometimes be enough of a bond to allow you to get the 'lowdown' on an applicant (particularly if it turns out you and your 'chum' now belong to the same professional associations). If you can establish rapport with the 'old boy', you might work the conversation around to something like, 'I'm considering this person for a crucial post, but I desperately need someone who'll be an asset to the team. Is there any way you can find out if this person's sound or if he/she had any problems?'

This is called 'networking'. The 'old boy' system works particularly well for military personnel, and school or college graduates, or any other group that feels any sort of continuing allegiance among its members.

Counterpart contact

Another good source to contact is the person who has the same title as you. If you're purchasing manager, contact the purchasing manager at the applicant's old employer. If you're in credit control, contact the credit control person. Start talking about the job. The chances are that the other person will realise your problems are just like his or hers and may open up with vital information about the applicant.

Employment: Conducting Meaningful Interviews

The decision to appoint is usually based upon the interview. You know it and the applicant knows it. Because so much depends on the interview, it can be a tension-filled meeting in which the applicant strives to present the best possible image while you strive equally to strip away the applicant's 'front'. This kind of situation, with both parties 'on guard', is not ideally suited to communication.

It would be a mistake to anticipate that in every interview you will get the applicant to 'open up' and reveal all. Nevertheless, it is still possible to conduct highly revealing interviews provided you approach them with a specific strategy and with clear goals in mind. This can be accomplished if the interview process is broken down into six minitasks:

1. Determine your interview goals
2. Develop an interview style
3. Understand the applicant
4. Plan the interview
5. Prepare specific questions
6. Know what to look and listen for.

1. Your goals

Before doing any interviewing, you need to be very clear about what your goals are, about what you want to get out of the interview. Obviously, you want to check on the *knowledge* and *skills* of the applicant. You want to find out what he or she is able to do.

Interviewers who *only* focus on knowledge and abilities, however, often miss out on the most important information

29

available from an interview, namely, *what kind of person* is sitting across the table. (See Task 1.)

You also need to know if the applicant will be committed to the job, if he or she will bring along energy and enthusiasm. Remember, an applicant who has the knowledge and ability to do a job, but who isn't committed to it makes a far worse employee than an applicant who doesn't know anything, but is committed enough to study day and night to learn the skills needed to do the work. Interviewing for knowledge and abilities is one thing. Interviewing for commitment is something else entirely. To get the right employee, you need to do both.

2. Develop an interview style

There are several different methods of conducting interviews which have become popular lately. Each is strategically aimed at getting the applicant to reveal as much as possible about knowledge and abilities as well as about personality.

The rapport interview

This interview rarely lasts more than 50 minutes. The idea is to follow a psychoanalytical approach in which the applicant is led to deeper and deeper levels of communication, and, along the way, reveals all.

The technique is based on rapport. The interviewer must quickly establish friendly communication with the applicant on a person-to-person basis. Once this is done, the interviewer honestly reveals one of his or her own minor personality traits. Because of the rapport that has already been established, the applicant now feels obliged to be equally revealing about a minor trait. Feelings of honesty, communication, and bond between the two people increase. Now the interviewer honestly reveals another bit of knowledge, ability, or personality trait that he or she has, and the applicant is encouraged to follow suit.

It could be described as 'opening up'. The interviewer takes off his coat and hangs it up. The applicant feels uncomfortable sitting there with a coat on, so he takes his off as well. The interviewer loosens his tie. The applicant relaxes and does likewise.

Obviously, it only goes so far and the applicant eventually refuses to 'completely undress' or completely reveal himself at some level. However, a skilled interviewer can use this technique to get enormous insights into the applicant in just a short period of time.

What works against this technique is the situation of the interview. Rapport requires calm and relaxation. An interview, on the other hand, is frequently fraught with tension. To overcome this some managers conduct this kind of an interview in a lounge situation, in easy chairs, or sitting next to the applicant on a sofa. Going out to lunch with an applicant can be useful where appropriate.

A word of warning, however. You can't conduct a rapport interview unless you really know yourself. You have to be willing to be really open about your own personality, knowledge, and abilities. No fudging! An applicant can tell in an instant if you aren't being honest and the effect is spoiled.

The biggest problem with this kind of interview is that it emphasises learning about the personality of the applicant. You can often quickly determine the person's commitment to a job. On the other hand, it is less useful in revealing an applicant's knowledge and skills for a job.

The multiple interview

This interviewing technique is literally based on exhaustion. There isn't one single interview. Rather there are three, four, or five interviews of the applicant—one right after the other.

Typically, an applicant is asked to report for an interview at 9am and is told the interview might last for several hours. He or she is then interviewed for about an hour by either someone from personnel or a boss who would not be the applicant's direct superior but who would work with him or her in an associate position. The applicant is not told there will be other interviews.

When this first interview ends, the applicant is introduced by the interviewer to the person who will be his or her immediate supervisor in the job and another hour-long interview is held. Again, the applicant is not told there will be other interviews.

At the end of this session, the applicant is introduced by the interviewer to a more superior boss and an additional hour's interview is held. Finally, this interviewer introduces the applicant to the divisional head, or some other higher-ranking supervisor, who takes the applicant out to lunch and there conducts a final interview.

The strategy has two distinct advantages. If any interviewer along the way feels the applicant will not qualify, he or she can end the process and eliminate the person by not progressing to the next step. The interview is ended cordially and the applicant never knows there were other interview hurdles to overcome. If the applicant does make it to the final stage, he or she has run the gauntlet and the top boss can make a job offer on the spot. Alternatively, the four interviewers can get together and compare notes before deciding whether to make a job offer.

The second advantage of the strategy is that four consecutive interviews (each of which covers much of the same ground) practically forces the applicant to reveal his or her true self. Weaknesses will pop out somewhere along the way, as will true personality traits. The applicant will be driven to self-revelation out of sheer exhaustion. It's the same technique that is often used by the police when questioning a suspect. The suspect must repeat his or her story over and over again to different people. When those people compare notes, inconsistencies glaringly stand out.

The problem with the multiple technique is that it is both time- and personnel-consuming. Three or more interviewers are required for each applicant. Therefore, it is used mostly for high-level positions.

Stress interviewing

This technique became popular a few years back when several high-level managers revealed that it was their method of identifying weaknesses in potential employees. In one case, a manager purposely cut half an inch off one leg of the chair in which the applicant sat for the interview. While the interviewer sat steadily watching from a large, comfortable seat, the applicant wobbled on a fragile wooden chair. This tended to distract and embarrass the applicant. The result was that applicants who had prepared themselves with 'cover stories' frequently forgot them, became confused, and in the process revealed their true personalities and job weaknesses.

Another boss would change the lighting in the room where the interview was conducted. She placed her desk in front of a large window from which the curtains had been removed. In addition, bright lights behind her were turned on. The effect was that while she could see easily, the applicant was blinded by the lighting and had trouble looking at her. Again the result was that the applicant felt distracted and tended to make revealing mistakes.

This technique relies on increasing the natural tension that occurs during an interview to the point where the applicant 'breaks' and reveals all. In some cases it is amazingly efficient, particularly where the job requires the employee to work under great stress. It does, however, have two drawbacks. Some applicants simply fall apart in such a situation, yet would make excellent employees. They end up talking gibberish, feeling foolish, and refusing to take the job even if it is offered.

On the other hand, there are some clever applicants who immediately understand what's happening and turn the situation around by commenting on the bad chair or the poor lighting and ultimately embarrassing the interviewer.

It isn't necessary to use one technique only. You can borrow some aspects from various methods, using those which work best for you. In the end, you'll probably end up simply asking questions and hoping for the best. Nevertheless, if you keep these techniques in the back of your mind, they may give you a little edge over the applicant.

3. Understand the applicant

In today's market-place, a manager must assume that the applicant is well acquainted with interviewing techniques. Some applicants even pay for coaching on how to handle interviewers. Most applicants regard getting a job as a kind of war in which the interview is the biggest battle. They come ready for it and unless you, as interviewer, are aware of what's going on, you can get blown right out of the water.

Turning the tables

The first thing that applicants are taught is to turn the tables

on the interviewer. As soon as the interview starts, an applicant using this technique begins asking you questions about
the company and about yourself. As you answer, they probe
deeper and deeper, continually nodding approval and smiling
as you answer. You have the feeling that things are going
well. Soon an hour has passed and you realise you've spent
the entire time talking about yourself and the company. You
haven't really learned much about the applicant, but you feel
you really do like the person and would therefore like to give
them the job.

You've been had. These applicants know that the quickest
way to make another person like them is to listen to that
person talk. They've got you to talk and they've listened.
They've become your friend, your confidant. Maybe you've
revealed a couple of problems and they've been sympathetic.
Who wouldn't like such an applicant!

What they've done is to turn the tables. Instead of you
interviewing them, they've interviewed you. If they want the
job, their nodding and smiling tells you you've passed and
they're more than halfway to their goal of getting taken on.

How to keep the tables from getting turned

A few years ago, when applicants were unsophisticated, this
wasn't much of a problem. But today, applicants at all levels
know this technique and managers must be on guard against
it. The way to avoid the problem is to recognise the fact that
we get information by *listening*, not by talking.

Often this is hardest when an applicant asks you about the
company right at the beginning of the interview. Yes, you will
need to tell the applicant about the company, but usually not
until the *end* of the interview. Until then you don't need to.
A good rule of thumb when interviewing is to speak 10 per
cent of the time and listen 90 per cent. One manager we know
has a special way of getting himself ready for an interview. He
goes into a corner and repeats to himself, 'Listen! Listen!
Listen!' Then he's ready to interview.

If the applicant asks a question, you can give a brief reply
which ends with another question. As we'll see shortly, you
can lead into questions that require long, thought-out answers.
As long as you follow the principle of listening, not talking,
the applicant can't turn the tables on you.

Spilling the beans

Applicants have also learned that the way to get hired is to tell the interviewer what he or she wants to hear. Therefore, today's modern applicant will almost invariably begin by asking you, 'What is the job you want me to do?' This seems a reasonable enough question. After all, how can you expect a person to interview for a position if they don't know what it is?

So you explain the responsibilities of the position. Along the way the applicant asks some specific questions about what the employee is supposed to do and how he or she will be expected to act. After five minutes or so the applicant nods that he or she understands what the job is and now you begin the formal interview. Even if you follow the 90/10 rule about listening and not talking, you find that this applicant is exactly what you want. It's incredible. The applicant's background and personality fits perfectly with the job. How can you not make an offer?

You've been had, again. The applicant began by finding out what kind of a person you were looking for, then moulded his or her background and personality to fit that person. You can be certain if you tell someone what you want, they will quickly become that person. The minute you let them know that vital information, you've 'spilled the beans' and you might as well forget the rest of the interview.

How to keep the beans in the pan

When applicants ask what the job is, they are really asking, 'What kind of a person are you looking for?' *Don't tell them.*

You're conducting the interview and you have options. You can simply ignore the question and refuse to answer it. If that seems rude or inappropriate, you can hand over a copy of the formal job description and give the applicant a few moments to read it. If the applicant asks questions about it, you can simply say, 'The description is comprehensive. The job is exactly what's written there, no more, no less. Now let's discuss your background.' Another strategy when the applicant asks about the job is to turn the question around. Reply by asking, 'What do you think the job is?' When the applicant replies you can then say, 'That's pretty close, now let's get on with the interview.'

Remember, *never reveal the kind of person you're looking for beforehand.*

4. Plan the interview

There are many different ways of actually planning the interview. However, we have developed a four-step procedure that works best in getting the applicant to reveal information about knowledge, abilities, and potential commitment.

1. Establish rapport
2. Go over the applicant's job history
3. Describe job being offered
4. Chat and close.

Establish rapport

To learn about the real person you must get beyond the superficial ritual of small talk, you must get the applicant to lower his or her defences, to open up, to tell you who and what they really are. For some people, this is very easy; for others, it is incredibly difficult.

Rapport is not just a fancy word. It's an important description that means 'intimate human contact'. It's not physical contact, but sympathetic person-to-person communication which some have described as psychological or even spiritual. Some call it 'empathy'. Whatever you call it, it means becoming intimate enough with another person so that they feel comfortable telling you information about themselves.

There are a few people who go through their whole lives never establishing true rapport with others. Yet it's not hard to accomplish. All that's necessary is first, to show the other person that you care about them and second, to open yourself up so they can see who you really are.

In the context of an employment interview, showing you care may mean asking if the person had any trouble in finding the interview location. Had it been difficult to park? Are they feeling up to an interview? Have they had a good day so far? Did they get a good night's sleep? Another more direct method is to explain carefully the interview process: that you will ask questions so you can learn about the other person, that you will take notes so you can be sure to remember what was said, that you want to give the other person every opportunity to express themselves and to be comfortable about what they say. It's mostly a matter of putting yourself in the other person's shoes so you'll get a feeling for what they're concerned about, and then being sympathetic.

Opening up can mean an amiable conversation during which you might share one part of your life, perhaps some one experience that happened to you that day. It could be your opinion of a song or a sports report you heard on the radio on the way to work; it could be a conversation you had with the girl down in the snack bar; it could be a revelation about the universe that came to you. The only critical thing is that it be revealing of yourself as a person.

Try some of these techniques the next time you meet anyone for the first time. It may take a few attempts before you get it right, but most people who are honest about themselves and who do honestly care about others can establish good rapport in less than five minutes with anyone they are meeting for the first time!

Go over the applicant's job history

A good way to start is to begin briefly with the applicant's education and quickly move to job history. This is where you can check for knowledge and skills as well as get a feeling for the person's ability to commit to a job. If you noticed any gaps or other pop-ups in the application, ask about them here.

When trying to learn about the applicant's knowledge, one manager we know uses an unusual technique: he *uses wrong information to get the right answer*.

While going over the applicant's job history, Peter would try to think about what he knew of the applicant's expertise. Almost always Peter could find some little bit of information he had tucked away about what the applicant had done, some part of what the applicant surely must know if that person indeed had the skills and knowledge claimed.

Peter would then take that fact he knew was correct and state it *incorrectly* to the applicant. If the applicant knew the subject, he or she would usually correct Peter politely. If the applicant didn't correct him, Peter would try to be sure the applicant had heard what had been said. He would repeat the *incorrect* statement asking, 'That's right, isn't it?'

If the applicant now agreed, Peter knew one of two things. Either the person didn't know what they were supposed to know *or* they were too shy to correct the potential boss's error. Either way, Peter would seriously consider eliminating the person.

Peter once was hiring an artist to do layouts for the company's annual report. He said, 'I'd like to use a serif type like Helvetica.' ('Serif' means a type style that has a cursive look to it. Any layout artist worth his salt knows that Helvetica is a *sans* serif type or one *without* serifs.) When the artist nodded agreement, Peter immediately knew the man was a fraud.

Describe the job being offered

This should be done *only* at the end of the interview. Often there is a game played at this point to try to find out the lowest salary the applicant will accept. The applicant, on the other hand, will try to keep from telling you this vital information if at all possible, and instead tries to find out the highest possible salary that you will pay.

If the game appeals to you, there are some phrases which can be helpful, such as, 'Are you anticipating a salary higher than your last job? How much higher?' Or, 'Give me a ball-park figure for what it would take to make you comfortable here.'

However, we have found that it works better simply to give a salary range for the job and then negotiate the actual salary, if necessary, once we've decided which applicant to accept. (It's important not to be penny wise and pound foolish. You don't necessarily want the cheapest applicant — you want the best.)

Chat and close

The interview begins when you meet the applicant and ends when he or she leaves. *All* the rest of the time is interview. Chatting casually after the formal interview has ended can often be the most revealing part. The applicant may now feel that the interview hurdle is over, and will relax and open up. You may learn more in five minutes of chatting than you did in 60 minutes of interviewing.

5. Prepare specific questions

It's a good idea to have a number of questions to ask written out in advance and an equally good idea to write down the answers the applicant gives. If you explain at the beginning of the interview that you will be taking notes to help you remember what the applicant says, there shouldn't be any objection.

Questions you must not ask

There are a number of items you must be careful not to ask about in interviewing. You should not ask women applicants questions that you would not ask men, for example, 'What arrangements have you made in case your children are sick?' or, 'Do you plan to start a family?' The information must be elicited indirectly during conversation.

Questions to ask

Trainability
'What jobs have you had which required specific training?'
'Tell me about the kinds of equipment (typewriters, machines, etc) you've worked on.'
'What kind of training would you like us to give you in this job?'

Flexibility and stature
'How would you handle working for two bosses?'
'If someone came to you with a complaint on the job, how would you handle it?'

Past work experience
'When we get in touch with your previous employers for references, what do you think they will tell us? Please explain.'

Personal outlook
'Describe what you expect to be doing during a typical day on the job.'
'If you could have been the boss in your last job, what things would you have changed?'
'What is your biggest concern in taking this job?'

Long-term outlook
'Describe a day on the job two years from now.'
'When you retire at the end of your career, what one accom-

plishment would you like people to remember you for?'
'What do you plan to be doing five years from today?'

6. Know what to look and listen for

Listening, as we've noted, is the key to interviewing. Here are
some of the things you want to listen for.

Three important answers you want to hear

*1. 'Both my long-term work goals and long-term life goals
are oriented towards the job you are offering.'*
Of course the phrasing will undoubtedly be different. But you
want to hear about the plans and hopes of the applicant. You
don't want to appoint a computer programmer who would
rather be acting on the stage. You don't want to put an
introvert in a salesperson's job. You don't want to stick an
independent thinker on an assembly line any more than you
want to put a routine worker in a group leader's job.

2. 'I'll "fit in" with the job.'
Again, you aren't going to be satisfied simply to hear the
applicant say these words. But if you listen carefully you'll be
able to hear whether or not the applicant can give this answer
by his or her conduct. What you are really judging is maturity.

The last thing you want to do is appoint someone who is
too insecure to make a vital phone call to a hostile competitor
or feels 'out of place' at an important meeting. You don't
want to hire someone who doesn't have the confidence to
'bawl out' a non-performing supplier or the assurance to
comfort a customer who didn't receive an order on time. You
also don't want to see the person you hire acting 'silly' with
his or her fellow employees, managers, or subordinates.

If the applicant's personal stature measures up to the job,
they will be comfortable in it. Their success will seem 'natural'.

3. 'I know how to produce results.'
Again, you have to listen 'between the lines' to hear this
answer. As mentioned earlier, in life there are the 'doers' and
the 'doddlers', and employees are drawn from both camps.
Since, ultimately, you are going to be concerned with results,
you want to know that this person knows how to get them.

You don't want to see the person you hire always 'appear' to be busy, but in reality never getting much done. You don't want to count on the new employee for a report that you need on 7 June only to learn on the 6th that it hasn't been started. You don't want excuses or explanations. You want results.

If the applicant is an achiever, his or her self-confidence will shine in the face of new challenges.

These, then, are the three answers that you want to hear — answers that will tell you that the applicant's goals are aligned with the job. Getting to them is usually just a matter of a few guiding questions and some intense listening. Remember, this is a positive test. You want to hear the right answers to get the right person.

Besides listening, there are many other items you will want to look for.

Self-confidence

Here is a quick test that a manager we know uses when engaging people to work in her restaurant. She is concerned that they have enough self-confidence to come across as pleasing even to disagreeable customers. She enters the interview and refuses to smile at the applicant.

It is the easiest thing for a person to *return* a smile, but if you don't smile first, it takes substantial self-confidence on the part of the other person to smile. This manager withholds her smile for just a bit at first. She sees how long it takes the other person to start smiling and become friendly. Then, of course, she returns the smile and opens up. But in the process, she's got a clue to the self-confidence of the applicant.

This technique is particularly useful for jobs involving customer service. Its drawback is that it tends to inhibit rapport.

Neatness

Observe the applicant's shoes, hair, and fingernails. Applicants know that the interview is important. If they are well groomed for it, it's a good sign. If they haven't cared enough to be neat for the interview, however, what does that say for their future commitment to the job?

Tension

The interview is a stress situation. Look for how well applicants handle that stress. Do they drum their fingers, bite nails, or exhibit any other uncontrollable mannerism? If they can't handle the strain of the interview, how will they manage the day-to-day stress of the job?

Responsibility

Note whether applicants are on time for their interviews. Do they blame others for past problems or accept responsibility themselves? (Watch out for blamers.) Do they run down former employers and associates? Blamers usually feel guilty for their own bad past performance.

Interviewer weaknesses to watch for

In addition to applicants' strengths and weaknesses, there are a number of interviewer weaknesses you also should be aware of in yourself.

Contrasting applicants

If one applicant comes in and is weak in all areas, the next applicant, even if he or she is just average, may seem super by contrast. Try not to judge applicants against others but against a set of criteria.

First impressions

First impressions are important. They can also be wrong. The applicant who stumbles when shaking hands can give you the impression he or she is a bumbler. But that impression may be totally wrong. Be on guard not to be swayed by first impressions.

Bad impressions

An applicant may have one overriding characteristic that gives you such a bad impression you overlook everything else. Maybe the applicant has bad breath. You can't stand the breath and so you grade the applicant down on everything else. It also works the other way. If an applicant is physically attractive, you may grade up everything else. Watch out for the single impression that overrides other judgement. (These are sometimes called the 'halo' and 'horn' effects.) Each of us has our own biases. When interviewing it's important to try to recognise them and work at not letting them sway our judgement.

Forgetting to listen

Many people tend to concentrate on the words being spoken. Don't forget to listen to the feelings behind the words. Listen to the person and not just to what he or she says.

Interviewing is more an art than a science. There are no perfect questions to ask, just as there are no perfect responses. Mostly, you are dealing with impressions and making judgements based on those.

If you follow the six minitasks outlined here, however, you should be able to conduct efficient interviews that in most cases will be highly revealing.

Task 6

Setting Employee Goals

About a decade ago a technique called 'management by objective' became extremely popular and was heralded as the final answer to managing. Essentially this technique said that to manage successfully, what was needed was to establish verifiable objectives for each worker. The employee would work towards those objectives and when they were achieved, both the worker and the manager would recognise this fact through some sort of mutually agreed verification. Then they could move on to other tasks. Multiply this by all the workers and managers and an entire company could move forward towards achieving its goals.

Today management by objective is commonly used in many companies. In this chapter we're going to look at it again, point out what we feel are some of its weak points, and suggest ways to improve on them.

Problems with management by objective

While on paper management by objective looks good, in real life we have found that it almost always does *not* fully work for three reasons:

Both managers and workers only give it lip service

The company says you must manage by objective, so at a set time the manager sits down with the employee(s) and they fill in the objective forms together. Then the forms are filed and everybody goes back to whatever they were doing before. No real attention is paid to the management technique.

If at the end of the period the objective is achieved, the

manager and worker(s) are congratulated, although the real credit is given to the management technique. If the objective wasn't achieved, then new objectives are set and the technique is credited with making clear that a problem existed. No matter what happens, the technique always comes off making the manager look like a winner.

The objectives are often unrealistic

In companies where the managers alone are allowed to set the objectives (which may be in the form of an annual production schedule), the workers often fail to achieve them simply because they are too difficult. The managers often write in their most optimistic work dreams without taking into account the workers' abilities and enthusiasm (or lack of them).

In companies where workers are allowed to set the objectives, usually little is accomplished because they are set too low. Workers are aware that promotions and bonuses hinge on successful performance, so they 'stack the cards'. They write in objectives they can easily attain, hoping to reap quick and easy rewards.

In companies where managers and workers sit down together, compromise is often the rule. Management's real goals may not be achieved, and workers still may feel that the objectives are too difficult.

Managers use the technique to stop managing

The real pitfall of management by objective for managers, however, is that it allows them to never again have to take the blame. If a supervisor wants to know how things are going, the managers can always pull out those objective sheets to demonstrate that they are on top of the job. If company objectives aren't met, it is always possible for them to say that company objectives were unrealistic.

Discussions always revolve around objectives (and sometimes their verifiability). No longer is the subject the managers, or their ability to manage. Rather it is the technique that is the subject. Thus managers can use the technique of 'management by objective' to get out of doing real managing.

Why management by objective can fail

In our opinion the real shortcoming of 'management by objective' is that the technique itself is essentially flawed. The flaw is that 'management by objective' is external and artificial. It doesn't actively engage the manager in the vital task of managing, but rather puts management 'on paper'. The essence of 'management by objective' is in following a procedure. If you follow the procedure, you can't lose. Thinking and vital interacting aren't always necessary.

At its most basic level, however, management is dealing with people. And people are not sheets of paper. No matter what we write down on our objective sheets, performance will hinge on individual effort. If we don't see to it that the effort is forthcoming, the worker – and the manager – will fail.

To put it another way, regardless of what 'management by objective' hopes to achieve, managing simply isn't mechanical. It's organic and interactive. It isn't something like a machine that you set up once, and leave alone, not coming back until it's finished. Managing is nurturing people.

Management through achievement

To correct the deficiencies of 'management by objective', we suggest a strategy we have named 'management through achievement'. An example will help to illustrate how it works.

The pitching game

We developed the following game for training new teachers to create situations that will help them become successful teachers. It is based on the familiar game of tiddly-winks.

In the game, second-year infants are asked to pitch little coloured discs (about the size and weight of pennies) into a small-necked basket. The children are placed on the 'pitching line' and the basket can be placed a marked distance away from them anywhere from two to seven feet. To illustrate the game to new teachers, at least three children are required, each playing the game for the first time, and each unaware of how others have played it before.

The first child who comes in is given five discs and told

that the goal of the game is to get three of the five discs into the basket. The basket is placed seven feet away. Typically the child will move to the pitching line and begin pitching discs. Because the basket is relatively small, it is almost impossible to get even one disc in at seven feet, let alone three. After a few sets of five, the child will usually get discouraged and stop playing the game.

Now another pupil is brought in. This one is told that the objective is to get the discs into the basket. But this time the child is told he or she may place the basket wherever desired, but as far away from the pitching line as possible. Typically, this child will start by placing the basket about half-way, perhaps three or four feet. At this distance, it's still hard to get the discs in, so the child will move the basket closer, to perhaps two feet. There, the game is easy. As soon as the child succeeds at two feet, he or she moves it to three. When there's some success at three, it is moved to four. Typically, children will move the basket to four or sometimes five feet before deciding it's too difficult and stop playing.

Finally the last child is brought in. The basket is placed on the two foot mark by the teacher and the child is told that the goal is to get three out of five discs in. This is normally achieved on the first or second try. At this point the child is praised and the teacher moves the basket to three feet. Again the child is told the goal is to get three out of five discs in it. Upon success there is more praise and the teacher moves the basket to four feet and then to five. At five feet, it is pretty hard, but most children are able to succeed rapidly, drawing on the experience they gained at closer levels.

Now it's moved to six feet out where it's really difficult. As long as the child shows enthusiasm, the basket is left there. However, as the child begins to get frustrated the basket is brought back to five or even four feet, where a few successful tosses restore confidence. Then it's moved back to six. Almost invariably the child soon achieves three out of five discs in at six feet. Now the basket is moved to seven feet out, where getting it in is next to impossible for a young child. But by now the infant is very confident in his or her ability and in many cases, the seven-foot level is achieved without a great deal more difficulty than the six-foot level.

Behind the game

New teachers are asked to notice what happened in this game. When the children were told that the goal was seven feet, nearly all of them simply stood at the pitching line and tried to throw the discs in. But because they didn't have the experience and confidence of achieving success at shorter distances, they quickly failed. When the child was allowed to set his or her own distance for success, invariably he or she selected a distance far less than the maximum attainable.

Only when the pupil was guided from a small achievement to ever greater ones was he or she eventually successful in getting the discs into the basket at the maximum distance.

This game shows prospective teachers that the key to building successful students is providing opportunities for them to first achieve and gain confidence in small ways. Simply expecting top performance right off won't work. Expecting them to do it on their own won't work. Only through a series of carefully guided situations where achievement is built on achievement can success be finally grasped.

Of course there are exceptions. Some children simply haven't the dexterity in the second year to get the discs in the basket even when it is only three or four feet away. They simply shouldn't have been selected for this exercise.

A very few others are smart and self-motivated. When faced with the basket seven feet away, they quickly realise that the key is gaining experience in tossing. On their own, without being coached, they move the basket closer until they achieve some success, then they move it farther and farther away until they are able to achieve seven feet. In a business setting such people would be known as self-starters.

The vast majority of students, however, are somewhere in between the ones who can't do the task at all and the ones who are sufficiently smart and motivated to work out how to do it on their own. It's to this vast majority that teachers learn to address themselves for most of their efforts.

For managers, the situation is not much different. To build successful employees, you need to provide an environment where your employees can build on ever-increasing achievements until their long-range goals, difficult though they may seem, become attainable.

That's why we call our strategy 'management through

achievement'. It's not simply a matter of setting goals or objectives. It's managing people so that they achieve many small goals on the way to larger ones. *It is in the creation of an environment where workers can achieve that the real management of people takes place.*

A strategic plan for management by achievement

There are five steps to setting achievable goals for workers. As a manager you need to act on all five:

Needs assessment

This can be as simple as your supervisor telling you, 'This is what we need'.

Or it can be more complex. It can be you as manager, your workers, and your supervisor all getting together and coming to a mutual decision on what's needed. Or it can be something that you are expected to decide all on your own. How needs assessment is carried out really depends on the type of company.

What needs assessment comes down to, however, is that it determines your own work goals.

Worker objectives

Once you know what your own goals are, you must determine objectives for your employees that will help you to realise these goals. In other words, you must figure out what tasks you want your employees to do that will result in your achieving your work goals. This is similar to the technique used in the standard 'management by objectives' plan.

Worker assessment

This is a vital step. From your knowledge of your employees' abilities, you must now make judgements regarding their chances of attaining the goals you've set up. In other words, you must match the person to the job. If an employee is a self-starter, perhaps you can simply explain the ultimate goal you have for them and if they concur, let them work out how to achieve it on their own. *Note:* It's a very rare employee with whom you can do this.

49

Like the second-year infants who lack dexterity, some of your workers may never be able to achieve certain objectives. You must not assign tasks which aren't achievable or frustration will result for all. In these cases, you must try to move such workers to tasks more suited to them.

In most cases, however, the worker can achieve success if properly motivated. That is, if he or she brings enthusiasm and energy to the job, the objective can be reached. Your goal is to bring out these qualities in the employees.

Setting achievable goals

This doesn't take long to do, but it can be the one task which requires your greatest concentration. You need to cut up the pie which is your ultimate objective. You need to cut it into easily swallowed slices. Each slice then becomes a separate goal attainable by the employee.

You need to figure out the *steps* which will lead to your final goal. That way the employee can achieve each step along the way until your final objective is met.

Note: Borrowing from the techniques of 'management by objective', you need to be sure that each goal is verifiable in a way that will be convincing both to you and to the worker.

Following through

Once you've set your objectives, the amount of time required to manage should be quite small. You see the employee and explain your short-range goal, explain its importance, and gain the acceptance and concurrence of the employee.

If the goal is really achievable there should be a fair amount of enthusiasm on the part of the employee. On the other hand, if the short-term goal is too difficult the worker will probably resist. You should be on the look-out for this resistance as it indicates an error in *your* planning. Now is the time to ask the worker for input and to *listen* to what is said. Now is the time to restructure the short-term goal until it is more realistic, more suited to the worker's ability.

Once the employee understands and concurs with the *achievable* short-term goal, you simply follow through. Keep an eye on what's happening to be sure the goal is achievable. Encouragement helps here. You should stay alert so that as soon as the employee achieves the short-term goal, you step in with praise. Then immediately go through the discussion process again with the next short-term goal, the next *step* in the process along the way to the longer-term goal. Remember to encourage and then praise for achievement.

In this way you manage your workers so that they move from achievement to achievement until they get to the ultimate objective. Ever-increasing achievements have built success for them and for you.

Dealing with problems

Problems can occur along the way. You may notice that the worker has slowed down, isn't making progress, appears *lazy*. It's time to reassess. Was the goal unrealistic? Are the worker's abilities and knowledge less than you originally thought? Is there an external problem facing the worker?

If the goal wasn't realistic, perhaps it should be broken down further into more easily achieved steps that are more in accordance with the worker's abilities and knowledge. In such a case after a period of frustration, it is vital that the worker achieves *quickly* so that he or she has the confidence to move on. Therefore this redesigned goal should be readily attainable.

If there's an external problem, refer the worker to appropriate counselling. A manager should never try to be a therapist.

An achievable goal example

Fred was a plant manager. He oversaw nine other managers at a factory which produced bathroom fixtures which were sold nationwide. Fred's sub-managers handled every level of production at the plant from the purchase of raw materials, through fabrication, into plating, and finally into packaging.

Fred's goals were largely set by the sales people. He had to keep production up to sales. (Occasionally he would have to cut production back to match lowered sales.)

Fred followed the 'management through achievement' plan.

1. First he would very clearly define his production goals for a specific period.
2. Next he would determine exactly what was needed from each area of production from the purchase of raw materials through to packaging in order to achieve those goals.

51

3. Next he would judge which of his workers (sub-managers) were best suited to achieving his goals. Sometimes this meant switching workers from one area of the plant to another. Sometimes it meant hiring a new employee and also transferring or laying off an old one.
4. Next he would break down the goals for each separate sub-manager into small parts. In some cases, monthly assembly line goals would be broken down into weekly or even hourly goals. The first goal might be 17 units an hour. When that was achieved, the next goal would be 18 units an hour. The ultimate goal might be 25 an hour.

   In another case reduced breakage might be the goal. Breakage would be first reduced from the current 7 to 6.5 per cent through specific safety and quality control procedures. Then the goal would be set at 6 per cent, and so forth.

   In yet other cases, his sub-managers' goals would be increased enthusiasm and creativity from their workers, evidenced by less absenteeism, fewer accidents, and greater productivity. Here specific morale-building techniques were to be introduced and evaluated one at a time.
5. Finally, he followed through. He sat down with each sub-manager and explained the immediate short-term goal. Fred worked hard to get his employees to agree with the goals. He knew the key to his success was working together. Where a manager saw that the goal could be achieved, that person usually concurred and was enthusiastic. Fred let the manager get started.

   Where the manager complained, Fred asked questions, re-evaluated, and usually came up with an easier goal. Where the manager wasn't enthused and didn't seem to care, Fred again asked questions, re-evaluated, and came up with a more challenging short-term goal.

   As work progressed, Fred watched. He adjusted goals where necessary, gave encouragement, and praised achievement. As short-term goals were achieved, new, mutually acceptable ones were set. In this manner Fred eventually was able to achieve his own goals set for him by the sales force.

Putting the strategy to work

The goal-setting strategy outlined in this chapter is based on people, not paper. It requires *active* management.

It means that you have to be aware of what's going on. On a regular basis (daily, weekly, monthly, or whatever is appropriate) you must check up so you know where the workers are on the road to achieving their goals. You must be alert for signs of 'lazy' behaviour which signals a problem with achievement, and you must take appropriate corrective steps.

Encouragement is required, as is praise.

What you should quickly discover, however, is how much extra time you have. Put this strategy into operation and you will suddenly find you are doing pure management. No longer are you doing your workers' jobs for them or having to constantly oversee them. Pure managing means fine tuning a smooth-running operation.

Remember, it's not how much time you spend, or how many reams of paper you fill writing down objectives, that makes the difference. Rather it's knowing that employees wish to succeed and will work hard if they can see a way to achieve.

Encouraging

Encouraging is a necessary follow-up once goals are established. Encouraging shows workers that you are alert and that you care. Note, however, that encouraging without first having established goals often backfires; workers may feel it is insincere.

What is encouraging?

'Encouraging' means stimulating people, giving them hope in their own progress, letting them know that they are on the right track. We have said that achieving is a natural desire and that it is the best motivator. People will work especially hard when they know they can achieve.

On any job, however, there are bound to be fairly long periods between achievements. Encouragement fills this gap. It is a kind of support that tells people that while they may not have yet achieved their goal, they are getting closer all the time.

Why encourage?

For most people it is far easier to give up than to continue with a hard task. This is particularly true where there is no real evidence of progress. This frequently occurs when a new employee comes into a company and every face he or she sees is a stranger. All the procedures are unknown. The work station is unfamiliar. It can be overwhelming and the person can get discouraged rather quickly.

Even an old employee starting towards a new goal can

experience dismay at seeing the enormous size of the task to be accomplished. Such a person may say, 'It can't be done', and give up before trying.

Both the new and the old employee may have achievable goals that they are working towards. However, particularly at the beginning, getting started can be the hardest step. A good manager will offer encouragement.

We all want approval, and encouragement is a kind of unconditional approval. It lets employees know that they are personally all right, that they are doing the right thing. As sentimental as it may sound, in a very real sense encouragement is the company's way of giving love, trust, and acceptance.

When to encourage

Proper encouragement of new employees, particularly during the first few days, can influence their attitudes towards work for years to come. Encouraging a new employee starts the person off on the right foot and keeps them on the right track. It is particularly useful during the first two or three days.

Another time to encourage is any time a worker starts a new task. Phrases such as, 'I'm sure you can do it,' or 'You're doing a good job there,' or 'We really appreciate what you've done for us in the past and we're glad you're the person handling this project,' can be helpful. The actual words don't count nearly as much as does the positive tone.

Encouragement can also be used as a stimulation when you see a worker slowing down (appearing lazy). Phrases such as, 'How are you coming along? Is there anything I can do to help?' or 'I really like what you've done thus far and can hardly wait to see the rest,' can be effective.

In addition to knowing when to encourage, it is also useful to know that encouragement works when specific types of behaviour occur. You can be fairly sure encouragement will help when a worker exhibits:

1. Slowness
2. Fear (at tackling a new task)
3. Insecurity (about acceptance either by the company, management, or other workers)

4. Weakness (doesn't currently have the ability or knowledge to complete the task, but can learn)
5. Depression (provided it doesn't have clinical causes).

Notice that in each of these cases the natural tendency might be to criticise, berate, or even 'bawl out' the employee for the behaviour. But you must understand the cause behind the behaviour is a lack of motivation resulting from insufficient achievement. Criticism of such behaviour, therefore, is inappropriate. Encouragement – giving unconditional acceptance, saying it's all right and that you believe in the person – is the correct antidote.

Sometimes the worker only needs to talk it out. *Listening* and simply nodding approval as an employee explains a problem or frustration can be an extremely effective means of encouraging.

Encouraging must always be positive

Remember that encouragement is a small reward. It must be freely given and it must make the receiver feel better about himself or herself. (Sometimes patting the person on the back or touching their arm while you're speaking to them helps get across the idea that you really do care.)

To summarise, there are three times when you want to encourage:

1. When a person is new on the job.
2. When someone is starting a new task.
3. When a worker slows down (appears lazy).

Overkill

Many people believe that if one pill works, a whole bottle will work a lot better. With encouragement, that's not the case. Encouragement has to be administered sparingly. It's a balm that must be hoarded to be applied only when there's a real need.

A great danger with encouragement is to go around giving it all the time. It's wonderful to be positive because it results in so much positive feedback for yourself. However, for the people on the receiving end, indiscriminate encouragement soon loses its value.

If you encourage every day, or even several times a day, people may begin wondering just what the value of that encouragement is. They may think that perhaps you're the sort of person who just wanders around with encouraging things constantly babbling from your lips. Hence the value of your encouraging is diminished, and when you really need it, it won't have the potency it should have.

Even worse can happen. If you encourage too much, employees may feel that you are insincere. They may begin to believe that you really don't care about them, aren't really trying to help them, but are simply engaged in a management trick, a kind of manipulation. The result can be a loss of trust which can disable your ability to manage. *Trust once lost can be very difficult to regain.*

Difference between encouragement and criticism

In Chapter (Task 9) we'll explore how to give criticism, but for now it's important to understand the difference between encouragement and criticism. Encouragement is *unconditional* acceptance of the worker. Criticism is *conditional* acceptance.

When you encourage, you say something like, 'I approve of you and your work'. On the other hand, when you criticise, you might say, 'I'll approve of your work if you improve this one area'. In criticism, approval hinges on a change of behaviour on the part of the employee. In encouragement, approval is unconditional.

Be sure you understand the difference and that you aren't inadvertently criticising when you mean to encourage.

People who are difficult to encourage

Some people are difficult to encourage. The classic example here is the egocentric person, the 'know-all'.

You walk up to this person and say, 'I think you're doing a good job there'. He or she turns to you and replies, 'Of course I am. What else would you expect?'

The natural tendency is to say to yourself, 'Well, pardon me for caring,' and storm away without giving any more encouragement.

Another version of this sort of person is the one who replies, 'Get off my back,' to your encouragement. This is the hostile worker, the one who by his or her words or tone warns you not to get close.

What is operating in both these cases is a kind of defence mechanism. Assuming there isn't a severe underlying psychological problem (which there might be and which you should not attempt to handle — remember, managers are not therapists), the worker is probably burdened by unexpressed fear or at least lack of confidence. However, instead of being open about the fear or lack of confidence, this worker turns the emotion into a kind of shield. Aloof or angry workers may actually be denying their own feelings.

When you offer encouragement, these workers may believe that you think they're having problems. But since they won't admit, even to themselves, that they might indeed be having problems, they deny the need for encouragement. In fact, they resent it.

How do you handle this? Sometimes you simply can't. This type of person may just not allow you to encourage. In such cases, you may need to wait until there is some actual achievement and then praise. (See the next chapter.) In some cases, however, you can encourage once you gain the trust of the individual. One way to do this is to reverse the situation. Instead of encouraging them, ask them to help you. One manager we know handles this difficult situation by first identifying something the worker has recently done successfully. Then she says something like, 'By the way, I'm having trouble with this. Can you help me?'

The worker now gives the manager aid for which the manager can then appropriately express thanks and even throw in a few words of approval. In this way the worker gets a small reward and feels good about his or her abilities or knowledge. In other words, the difficult worker learns to accept encouragement.

Encouragement is one of the best tools a manager has. It doesn't take long to do and when used appropriately can yield enormous results, not the least of which is that it even makes the person giving it feel better!

Praising

Praising is a vital part of managing. Giving praise is acknowledging the achievement of a specific goal or a desired behaviour. It lets workers know that you recognise their work. Your recognition puts a stamp of approval on their achievement.

Praising should not be underrated. It motivates employees to keep on achieving. Some managers feel that if you don't praise good work, you'll have to make up for it in some other way, such as giving bonuses or salary increases. Praising, however, can't be indiscriminate. There are established rules which must be followed.

Rules for praising

Give praise only for the achievement of a specific goal

You have to be careful. If you go to Judy to praise without first checking to see that there's been achievement, you set yourself up to lose. Suppose you casually remark as you pass by, 'That's really good work.'

Judy may turn and ask, 'What is?'

In other words, she didn't know she had achieved anything. Was there something she missed that deserved praise? Why how wonderful, she may be thinking. Now tell me what it is that I've done so I can feel good about it, too.

Since you weren't watching carefully, you now scramble, looking for something to praise. 'Why, I just meant your, well, your regular work.'

'But I just broke this item I'm trying to assemble.'

'Well, of course, I mean your day-to-day work, not necessarily your work of the moment,' you say, feeling rather embarrassed.

Judy now feels let down. She hadn't really done anything praiseworthy. What's worse, she now may feel that though you are well-intentioned, you aren't alert. She had thought you were a careful manager aware of what she is doing. Now you've let her know that you aren't as watchful as she thought. In the future she may let a few things slip.

Praise is recognition of good work. The good work must be there for the praise to be justified. That means that you must take the time to be aware of just where people are on the road to achieving their objectives, so that on the day the objective is achieved, you are there with your praise. A super manager keeps a sufficiently careful watch, knows when small goals are achieved on the road to bigger ones, and is able to give praise along the way.

When praise is appropriate, it tells workers that you are alert to their progress and appreciate it. This makes them feel important, needed, and worthwhile. It builds their self-esteem, and that is what will carry them forward to greater achievements.

Praise must be appropriate for the achievement

Insincere praise

If Jim completes the sale of a small insurance policy, his manager wants to praise him for his efforts. However, if the manager goes over the top and says, 'That's terrific, that's the best sale in the world! You're dynamite as a salesman! I bet you feel proud!' Jim, of course, is bound to be suspicious. He just sold a £1,500 term assurance with a £70 premium. If this is how his manager reacts, then the manager must be:

1. Insincere
2. Desperate for business (so why is Jim working there?)
3. Manipulative (trying to praise Jim because he wants some hidden thing in return).

Jim may have been feeling modestly proud of his small achievement. Now, he may feel embarrassed by it. Instead of making him feel good, feel successful, his manager may have made him feel suspicious and used.

Insufficient praise

There is, of course, the other extreme – giving insufficient praise for a major accomplishment. Jim sells a group life assurance policy to a company with 130 employees. The first year's premium is £20,000. He comes back beaming.

His manager glances at the policy, mumbles, 'Good work, keep it up,' and goes on with whatever he had been doing.

He's taken the wind out of Jim's sails. This was an outstanding sale, perhaps a once-in-a-year occurrence for him. He's thrilled by it. He sees it as a real achievement, as the attainment of a significant sales goal, as a measure of his success.

His manager has just shown him how wrong he is. The faint praise suggests that it was just a normal sort of sale, the kind that's to be expected of him, no big deal.

Jim is likely to either become frustrated, feel defeated, and slow down *or* to go to someone else (possibly a competitor), tell that person what he's done, and there get the kind of praise he feels he deserves.

Remember, when workers achieve they not only feel they deserve praise, they demand that the praise be appropriate to the achievement.

Praise must be appropriate to the person

Some people deserve praise, want praise, but don't know how to handle it. Imagine taking a shy person to a restaurant on their birthday. At the end of dinner, by arrangement, out come all the waiters and waitresses carrying a cake and singing 'Happy Birthday'. An extrovert might shine on such an occasion, but a shy person may feel humiliated. It's not that a celebration wasn't called for. The point is that the celebration should be geared to the individual's temperament.

Alice is an extrovert. She's totally open, constantly talking with her co-workers. She's just attained an important goal. You go out and praise her achievement in front of her co-workers. Alice beams in delight.

Alicia is an introvert. She is quiet, seldom speaks unless first spoken to. She, too, has just attained an important goal. You ask her into your office or take her aside and quietly tell her how pleased you are with what she's accomplished. Alicia also beams in quiet delight while looking around to be sure no one has overheard.

You've matched your praise to the individual. But reverse the situations – praise Alice in private, Alicia in front of her co-workers – and see the damage you could do.

The difference between praise and encouragement

As we said in the last chapter, encouragement is the unconditional approval of a person's work. Encouragement isn't earned, it is given gratuitously. It shows that you want people to succeed, that you have the confidence that they will succeed. It gives them the courage to move forward through what might be a difficult task.

Praise, on the other hand, is approval of an achievement. It is *always earned*. Never give praise gratuitously. Never praise someone who hasn't achieved something. Praise shows recognition. It lets people know that you are alert to their achievements. It lets them know that the company appreciates what they've done. It's the reward that makes all the work possible.

Praise as the successful completion of a task

Praise is also the signal that terminates the progress to a completed goal. The worker does the work, then brings it to you. By praising, you let them know that you and the company approve and agree that the objective was achieved. This allows the person to put that old goal past them and start towards a new one.

Praise, like a smile, is free. It costs nothing to give, yet can bring enormous returns. We have never met a successful manager who didn't know how to praise. We also have never met a successful manager who didn't follow the three rules of praising.

Criticising

It's very important that managers understand what criticism should not be before attempting to use it. Criticism should *not* be:

- ☐ Bawling out another person
- ☐ Being critical of another person
- ☐ Reprimanding for bad performance
- ☐ Being negative.

This may seem surprising since the word 'criticise' has such negative connotations in our language. To most people, it implies something quite bad. Many assume, in fact, that to criticise means to be negative in dealing with others. This is unfortunate, because such 'bad criticism' is almost always counter-productive.

An employee is often worse after negative criticism than before. A manager may intend to improve a worker, but after bad criticism is chagrined to see that the work performance or behaviour actually slips. Some managers, having seen this undesired result of bad criticism, have even begun to think that there is no real place for criticism in managing people.

Nothing could be further from the truth. Criticism is a way of correcting the behaviour or work performance of an employee. But to be effective, it must be handled properly. Criticism is like a stick of dynamite. It has the potential for either great good or great harm.

Working with criticism, like working with dynamite, takes care and understanding. It is important to understand the difference between negative and positive criticism and know how to give constructive criticism. It is also important not to have unrealistic hopes for what criticism may accomplish. It can indeed make significant changes, but it isn't a miracle cure.

The goal of criticism

The goal of criticism is almost always to improve behaviour or work performance or both. There is normally a positive objective.

Thus we usually end up criticising employees or workers who aren't doing what they are supposed to. Henry isn't producing his quota of sales, so we criticise (we try to get him to increase production). Phyllis isn't assembling enough product and we criticise her (we want her to assemble faster). Sally isn't spending enough time at her work, so we criticise (we want her at her work station, not at the coffee machine). In other words, our goal in criticising is to get the worker either to improve work performance or behaviour (or both).

Problems with criticism

Problems usually arise, however, when you lose sight of your goal for the criticism because of your own personal feelings. Your supervisor may have just pointed out that your production is down. How can that be, you wonder, until you look around and see Sally chatting with a friend by the coffee machine. That's the reason! You storm over and criticise (bawl out) Sally.

Your goal was to get Sally to stop taking so many breaks. The result, however, is that you probably only antagonised her, so that in the future she'll be tempted to do the opposite of what you want.

Sometimes criticism isn't angry, but just awkward. Henry's sales are slipping. You quickly see that the problem is that he isn't spending enough time 'cold calling' (making blind phone calls to potential clients). You aren't angry, you just want to help. So you go up to Henry and say, 'Your problem is you're not reaching out to the clients.' Henry looks at us, retorts, 'I don't have a problem, you do!' and takes the rest of the day off.

Your friendly criticism was taken the wrong way and produced quite an unexpected and opposite result. Thus even when you're not angry, your criticism may turn out to be negative and work against you.

Negative criticism

If ever a management technique required a clear strategy, it's criticising. In no other area are you as likely to accomplish the opposite of what you want. Wrong or negative criticism is often simply the 'natural' thing to do. You may simply be inexperienced in knowing how to give constructive criticism. Sometimes good criticism just never gets expressed.

Therefore, let's take a moment to look at what negative or wrong criticism really is. We've already suggested it can be counter-productive. Now let's see why that happens. To do this, we'll take an example from the world of animals.

Negative criticism in training animals

From television or visits to aquatic parks and circuses, you're probably somewhat familiar with techniques used by animal trainers. These techniques mainly involve positive reinforcement for good behaviour without undue criticism of bad. For example, the dolphin performs the trick and is given a fish as reward. If the dolphin fails to perform, the trainer scolds modestly, encourages, and then urges the dolphin to try again. It tries, performs, and then gets its reward.

A dog is supposed to jump through a hoop. It tries and fails. The trainer comforts the dog, then carefully leads it through the hoop by hand, finally urging it to try again. The dog tries and this time succeeds and is immediately rewarded with a treat.

Notice that there is little negative criticism in these examples. The technique is positive. When the dolphin doesn't perform, the trainer might say a word of scolding to acknowledge that he or she has seen the bad performance, but immediately the animal is encouraged to try again. When the dog doesn't perform, the trainer shows it exactly what's required and then urges it to try again.

Both cases are a form of criticism. Neither the dolphin nor the dog gets its reward when it doesn't perform. It may even be mildly scolded. But at no time is either the dolphin or the dog made to feel that it is a bad animal. There is no attack by the trainer on the animal itself. The trainer always keeps in the forefront of his or her mind the goal, namely that the animal should perform the trick.

65

We have been told by trainers that if someone who is trying to teach an animal a trick severely scolds it or even hits it, the animal is likely to become so defensive that it will be unable to perform the trick again that day. Repeated negative criticism over even a short period of time can prevent the animal from being able to perform for a much longer period.

In other words, negative criticism causes the animal to lose confidence in both the trainer and in its own abilities. This in turn results in an inability to perform the desired goal.

Negative criticism in changing people's behaviour

But what about people? We are certainly far more sophisticated than dolphins or dogs.

Yes we are, but like animals, we react adversely to negative criticism of any kind. Consider your own behaviour. If you've just completed a difficult task and someone comes up to you and says, 'Finished at last, eh? Man, are you slow. You should be able to go twice as fast,' are you likely to receive that person's criticism warmly and act positively on it?

On the other hand, suppose the same person says, 'Congratulations on finishing. You did a good job. I wonder if next time we couldn't manage it a fraction faster.' Are you more likely to strive harder now?

Personalising negative criticism

People, like animals, tend to take negative criticism to heart. It really doesn't matter if someone is only criticising their work. If it's negative, they *always* assume the comments are personal.

A manager moves up to a worker and says, 'Say, Jim, your work looks terrible.' Jim turns to a fellow worker and says, 'Did you hear that? He said I look terrible.' Jim 'heard' the negative remark as a criticism of himself rather than his work.

A manager says to Jill, 'Say, have you got an untidy desk!' Later at lunch that day Jill says to a friend, 'Can you imagine the nerve of that manager calling me a slob!'

Again, although the criticism was work-directed, the worker took the negativism personally and 'heard' the remark as a personal criticism. Of course, implicit in both remarks was the manager's goal to criticise bad work or behaviour and thereby get the worker to improve or clean up her desk. But that's not the message that got across.

When you're negative, the *only* thing that gets across is the negativism. Specific work or behaviour comments are brushed aside by the listener. Only the negativism comes across and that comes across personally.

Try this little test. Read the next paragraph and then, before moving on, try to determine exactly what the manager wants.

As Peter puts down the phone, the manager walked up and said, 'Caught you! It's people like you who are keeping this company in the red. There's a pay phone outside...use it!'

What's happening here? What is the manager's goal? What has he accomplished?

Peter's reaction is anger. As it turns out, Peter had just made a phone call to his girl friend to ask her out to dinner that night. However, the company had a firm policy against personal calls.

The manager was understandably upset. Peter was on the phone ostensibly doing business, while actually making a date. The manager's goal was to get Peter to stop making such calls. However, what got across was the manager's anger and his negative comments. As a result, Peter never got the message that the problem was his personal phone calls. Rather the message was that the manager had personally insulted him. In the future Peter might either make personal phone calls as a matter of defiance (or disguise them more cleverly).

The power of negative criticism

Because negative criticism tends to be taken personally, even if it's directed at work performance, it is extremely powerful. A tiny, tiny bit of negative criticism can totally devastate someone.

An example of this was noted in the late 1960s at San Francisco State College (now California State University of San Francisco) in the marking of English papers of students who had failed English proficiency tests.

Traditionally the marking was done by teaching assistants. They would mark the papers in red ink, indicating areas that were wrong as well as areas that needed improvement. The idea was that this written criticism was intended to improve the writing of the students.

However, when the student writers were given back their

papers, allowed to read them, and then immediately asked what the criticism said, few could remember anything that had been written in the red ink except the impression it gave them that they personally were poor writers. *This was true even in cases where the criticism had been entirely complimentary!*

As an experiment the teaching assistants were now instructed to write in blue ink. Again, as soon as the students had read their papers they were asked what was said. Now the majority clearly remembered the criticism, even if it had been negative.

The colour of the ink determined how responsive the students were! There was nothing magical about blue ink. What had happened was that over the years of attending school, students had learned to associate red ink with negative comments. When the students got back a paper with red scribbling on it, they immediately assumed it was negative criticism that would make them feel bad. As a result they just turned it off. They turned it off so acutely, in fact, that they couldn't even comprehend what had been written, even if it was positive.

The whole point, of course, is that even the smallest indication of negative criticism is taken personally and puts a person into a defensive reaction that obscures the content of what's being said.

If this is the case with written work, it is even more so with oral criticism. Toastmasters International, an excellent organisation dedicated to helping people overcome the fear of speaking in public, has an evaluation period as part of each member club's regular meeting. Members give speeches and then during this 'evaluation' period, other members comment on how well the speakers did. However, it's an unwritten rule that no matter how bad the speaker was, the evaluator will always begin the evaluation by commenting on some of the positive things the speaker did, and throughout the evaluation continue occasionally to make positive comments.

The point is that it's vitally important that the speaker hear positive things about his or her performance. This confirms in the speaker's mind that the evaulation is not a personal attack and that, on the whole, the speaker is a worthwhile person who, through a bit of work, can improve performance or behaviour.

We've seen first-hand how disastrous results can occur when this policy is not followed. At one meeting we attended, a fairly good speaker gave a mediocre talk. During evaluation, the evaluator immediately began criticising everything from the speaker's use of voice modulation and hand movements to his topic organisation. We agreed with all of the evaluator's comments, though not his method of presenting them.

Afterwards the speaker was asked what he thought of the evaluation. We still remember his words. He said, 'He told me that I'll never be able to give public talks. This is my last meeting. I'm off!'

The speaker hadn't 'heard' one word of the evaluator's criticism. The comments, all relatively minor, had been obscured by the method of presenting them. All that the speaker got out of it was the feeling that he, personally, was bad. Instead of helping, the evaluator had made the speaker feel diminished. He had, in fact, almost destroyed this person's self-confidence in terms of public speaking. It took much sympathetic and careful encouragement to get the speaker to stay with the club and to continue to improve his public speaking.

No negative criticism

A little negative criticism goes a very long way. It goes so far, in fact, that our goal in this section is to convince you never to use it. So much more can be accomplished with positive criticism, and the dangers of producing an undesired reaction are so strong, that the rule to follow is simple: *never give negative criticism.*

In fact, a good way to remember it is to convince yourself that there is only positive criticism. If it's not positive, then it's something else. If you just keep in mind that when you are negative, you are not in any way achieving your goal of improving worker performance or behaviour, then you're halfway to being a good critic.

Aversion therapy

Before leaving negative criticism, a word must be said about a kind of negative criticism that has become popular in recent years called 'aversion therapy'. Here a person is subjected to intense negative feelings about something in order to convince him or her to avoid it. For example, a smoker may purposely be made sick from inhaling smoke. The idea is that every time in the future that the person thinks of smoking, he or she will remember being sick and refrain from smoking.

Aversion therapy may have its place in a controlled environment when administered by people specially trained in its use and for a defined and specific problem (such as conquering the smoking habit or overcoming alcohol addiction). But it has no place in the manager's bag of management techniques.

A manager who tries to extrapolate aversion therapy from the medical setting to the workplace is asking for nothing but trouble. The results may be poor performance, worsened behaviour, and probably loss of personnel. Remember, a manager should never be a therapist.

Positive criticism

As we've said before, there is a natural desire to succeed. We all love success, in fact we thrive on it. Positive, or good, criticism makes use of this desire. Positive criticism expands a worker's horizon and shows the road to achievement.

Working with rather than against

The essence of positive criticism is that it engages the worker's cooperation in improving and then shows how the improvement can be accomplished. In other words, with good criticism you are on the worker's side. You want someone to succeed and you help them so that they can.

An example is this illustration of a good teacher. Jill is having trouble with her maths. She just can't do long division, and has just turned in a paper on which every answer was wrong. Jill's teacher uses good criticism. The teacher does *not* bawl out Jill for doing badly. The teacher does not say there is something wrong with Jill for having failed with each problem.

Rather, the teacher sits down with Jill and tries to help her understand how to do the computation. She might start out by being sympathetic. 'Isn't it a shame that the mark is so poor when you worked so hard. You are an intelligent person. You can be a strong student. Perhaps it's just a little matter of not quite understanding how to do the problems. Why don't we go over a few together? Perhaps we'll see exactly where the trouble is.' The teacher goes through several computations step-by-step until Jill understands the method of long division. Then the teacher says, 'There, I knew you could do it. It was just the little business of moving that decimal.'

Jill leaves feeling terrific. Of course she could do it. She knew how all along, except for that little problem with the decimal. And now that she has that under control, there's no question of her success. She's even anxious to take the next test to show off her long division prowess.

Three elements of positive criticism

There are three important features of positive criticism that you should notice in this example:

1. Notice that the nature of positive criticism in this school setting was constantly to *reinforce the value of the person*. Jill is a good person, a good student. The problem is shown to be external. The difficulty has to do with decimals. If Jill wants to get angry, she can get angry at the decimal point. That is what caused her problem and made her slip up.

   The same holds true with workers. Positive criticism begins by assuming the worker *wants* to succeed and *can* do so. The problem is something external that the employee can deal with. Once this has been established, then the employee has the confidence to move forward to correct whatever it might be.

2. Notice also that the problem that needs to be corrected is *always referred to as a* minor *difficulty*. There's an important reason for this. *Major* problems often don't have solutions. Minor problems, on the other hand, can *always* be solved. Making the difficulty 'minor' automatically reinforces the belief that it can be overcome.

3. Finally we should notice that positive criticism always *engages the cooperation of the person being criticised.*

It's not the teacher against the student, the manager against the worker. It's both working together to solve a common, solvable difficulty.

Does it work?

Now that we have some idea of what positive criticism is, the big question becomes, does it work?

Yes it does work, but don't expect to fully believe it yourself until you have a chance to try it out. In fact, part of the difficulty in believing that good criticism does work comes from the fact that it doesn't really fit the mould of what most of us consider as a definition of criticism.

As noted at the beginning of this chapter, with positive criticism we:

- ☐ Never bawl out another person
- ☐ Are never critical of the person
- ☐ Never reprimand
- ☐ Are never negative.

It can be hard getting used to this new way of handling things, but the results are certainly worth it.

Using positive criticism

Jenny is a secretary whose responsibilities include answering the phone, taking dictation, and writing letters. She has an excellent telephone manner and seems able to handle the dictation without difficulty, but there are frequently many misspelled words in the letters she writes. Jenny just can't spell.

She has just handed you the second letter for signing this morning and without even reading it, you can see that there are two glaring errors in the first line. Our immediate and natural impulse is to shout at Jenny, but we know this is pointless. It won't improve her spelling and will undoubtedly damage your ability to work with her. In fact, it might go so far as to reduce her efficiency in other areas.

Instead, you calm down. When there is a quiet moment, you call her aside. First, you reassure her about her overall performance. She's a good employee and does nearly all of her job well. She's very good on the phone and takes dictation accurately. There is, however, one small area that needs some improvement and you're quite confident she can deal with it. You might even ask if she knows what you're talking about.

Of course she knows. Jenny is well aware she can't spell.

If she knows, but isn't improving, perhaps it's because she doesn't understand the value of correct spelling. So you point out why good spelling is essential. Letters represent the company to others. If the letter has misspellings, it looks sloppy and inefficient and then, so does the company image. Further, Jenny undoubtedly wants to succeed at her present job and be promoted. The inability to spell will surely slow her down. Therefore, it's to everyone's advantage if she simply gets over this minor problem of not spelling well.

Jenny looks embarrassed. She doesn't know how to improve her spelling. Of course, you think to yourself, if she knew how to spell better, she would. So now you see to it that she learns how. As a start, you provide a pocket dictionary so that she can look up the words she's unsure of.

You allow her extra time for a while to type her letters so that she can use the dictionary. For a short period you might even arrange to have another secretary (who knows how to spell) check Jenny's work. You might even arrange for Jenny to take a local evening class in spelling improvement.

Will Jenny spell better? Why shouldn't she? You want her to. She wants to herself. And now you've provided the means for her to improve.

Avoid backsliding

You may be tempted to say, 'But that's not criticism. Simply working with Jenny never told her she was doing something very *badly*. There wasn't even any *punishment* for the letters she originally did poorly.'

This sort of thinking is simply backsliding. You've seen that negative criticism doesn't work, yet it's hard to shake the idea that criticism must be negative. So when you see positive (good) criticism at work without any negativism, you think it isn't criticism at all.

You must concentrate on your goal. Your goal is to correct and improve worker performance or behaviour. If doing it this way works, then it is criticism. A little trick is always to avoid the following words when criticising a worker:

Key words to avoid when criticising
   Bad
   Poor
   Wrong
   Punishment
   Inadequate
   Problem
   Loser

The difference between criticism and reprimand

It's important to understand that there is a difference between criticising and reprimanding. Criticism is typically used when we find someone doing a task or behaving incorrectly. It is used to *inform* the person and engage their *cooperation* to do better.

Reprimanding, on the other hand, is used *after* criticism has been given a chance. You have used positive criticism; the person now understands how to do the task or how to behave correctly, but for some reason refuses. Reprimanding is now letting the person know that they are guilty of an infraction. (We'll discuss it more in the next chapter.)

How to give constructive criticism

You need to be sure that you understand the procedure for giving good criticism. It isn't difficult and anyone can do it. It's just a matter of being aware of these five simple steps:

1. *Understand your goal.* What behaviour or task do you want improved? To what level do you want it improved?
2. *Reassure the worker that this is not a personal attack.* It's the behaviour that needs changing. Find and compliment the good work the person is doing, point out that you know the person can succeed, that he or she is basically a good worker.
3. *State that you have a* minor *but important concern.* Show confidence that the person can indeed improve

and correct the situation.

4. *Determine how the problem can be corrected.* Discuss this with the worker and gain his or her cooperation.
5. *Reassure the worker.* Tell him or her that all will be well and to keep trying. In other words, point out that every opportunity still exists for success.

Reprimanding

We reprimand when someone has done something wrong. Johnny is caught with his hand in the biscuit tin. We give him a reprimand. Susy came to the dinner table without first washing her hands. She is reprimanded. Implicit in reprimanding is the understanding that both Johnny and Susy knew what was expected. They understood the correct behaviour that was expected of them, but for some reason they did otherwise.

It's essentially the same in the workplace. John is late for work every day. If, in fact, he thoroughly understands that he is expected to be on time, then a reprimand may be in order. Susan makes a shambles of her work area. If she understands that, because customers come through where she works, the area is expected to be neat, then a reprimand may be in order.

The goal of a reprimand is to let the worker know in no uncertain terms that:

- ☐ behaviour or work (or both) is unacceptable
- ☐ what is acceptable work or behaviour
- ☐ further infractions will not be tolerated.

Criticism before reprimand

Normally a reprimand will be preceded by criticism. As we said in the last chapter, the goal of criticism is to help and inform. An employee isn't achieving because he or she really doesn't know how. So you give constructive (positive) criticism which shows the person the path to success. On the other hand, if it is clear that the person already knows what to do (either in terms of behaviour or work) and persists in not doing it, then it's a different matter.

It's important to understand that there is a thin line between reprimanding and criticising. If you're not really sure that the person understands what's expected, then you should always strive for constructive criticism. *When in doubt, constructive criticism should always be used before reprimanding.* In fact many managers *never* reprimand. They always assume that a failure to do work correctly or to maintain correct behaviour stems from a lack of understanding.

What is reprimanding?

Reprimanding, like criticism, has negative connotations. It tells us that we've done something wrong. From childhood we tend to associate it with being bad.

This is unfortunate, for when people are told that they are bad, they tend to believe it. If you tell someone that he or she is a bad worker, then as their supervisor you have just defined his or her *value* as a worker – bad. If they weren't bad before, they certainly are going to lean that way now. After all, if your words are to be believed, it's what you expect of them.

The problem is that most people have been conditioned to think of being reprimanded as being attacked. *You* are not doing what's expected of you, hence there must be something wrong with *you*. (In fact the attack may be on the behaviour, not the total person. We don't like what you *did*, not we don't like *you*. But that's not the way it usually comes across.)

Bad reprimanding

Bad reprimanding, like bad criticism, makes a person feel diminished, a 'bad person'.

'This is the third time this week you've been late, John. What's the matter with you? You need to get your life in order: get up or start out earlier. You can't expect to arrive late all the time and not have people angry with you.'

People are very sensitive to your expectations of them. If John thinks you are 'angry' with him, that you see his life as 'out of order', then maybe that's the way he will act in the future. And since a person with a life out of order and people angry at him can't really be expected to come to work on time, maybe he won't in the future.

As with bad criticism, bad reprimanding is counter-productive. An attack on a person only makes that person less eager and less able to perform as you want. At times it may make your ego feel a little better, but a scolding simply isn't going to get the results you want. (And, after all, what you are ultimately concerned about is results.)

Good reprimanding

The key to good reprimanding is expectation. If you expect bad work or behaviour, very likely you'll get it. If you expect good work or behaviour, then that's the result you're most likely to see.

When you give a constructive reprimand, behind it must be your assumption that you are dealing with a good person who can and will correct the offending behaviour or work. If you don't believe in the person, then you really have no business reprimanding. If you think the person is bad, all you'll be doing is reinforcing this belief, making things worse for the person and, very likely, worse also for yourself.

If you have a positive attitude towards a worker who is not performing as required, if you believe the person wants to succeed, then your reprimand will take a constructive form.

Susan's work area is a mess. You go to Susan and say you know she's aware that because of her sensitive location in front of customers, it's vital that her work station be kept neat and tidy. Yet, three times this week the station hasn't been that way.

'We have confidence in you and your abilities and believe you can succeed in the company. However, one of your job requirements is a neat work station. If you can't maintain tidiness, then that job requirement isn't being fulfilled and we may not be able to continue you in this job.

'It's just a simple matter of neatness, which can easily and quickly be corrected. I know you're a good worker and you'll take care of it.'

The good or constructive reprimand begins and ends on a positive note.

Three parts of a constructive reprimand

There are three essential elements that must be present in a good constructive reprimand:

1. The person must be made to feel that it is only a single identifiable aspect of the work or behaviour that is the problem. It's not *the person* that's wrong. It's one *small* thing he or she is doing.
2. The worker must believe that the problem is correctable and that once corrected, everything will be well again. In other words, once the problem is taken care of, it will once again be possible for the worker to move forward with achievements in the company. (If this possibility isn't there, why should the worker correct the problem?)
3. The employee must understand that there will be consequences if the problem is not corrected.

Consequences

While it is important to point out the need for compliance when a worker is not performing, it is equally important to underline the fact that continued lack of performance will have a consequence. In other words, only if the worker fully understands that you will be forced to do something (such as write a poor annual assessment, transfer, penalise or dismiss them) is the reprimand likely to have teeth.

Making consequences for bad performance has two benefits. First, it makes the worker responsible for solving the problem. Second, it makes sure that the worker understands that it's his or her problem, not yours. It's important that the problem be identified as the worker's. Giving consequences allows you to be very frank with the worker. 'Here's the job. You know what's expected. It's up to you to do it or you'll have to pay the price.'

The key to remember about consequences is this rule: *workers must be made to understand that they are responsible for performance.*

If they don't perform, undesirable consequences are inevitable.

79

When to reprimand

A reprimand should be given only if the offence is either serious or repeated.

John is late once in a while, but his work is complete and on time. No reprimand is needed. Just look the other way. John may need the flexibility of occasionally coming in late in order to maintain his work load.

Susan's desk is occasionally a mess, but she cleans it up right away if any customers are present and always speaks to them in a friendly and warm manner. Forget the desk. Perhaps some of her work is difficult and frustrating for her and that is reflected once in a while in her work station's appearance. As long as she's getting the job done, overlook an occasional lapse in neatness.

Simply being aware that some problems are occasional and are not serious can save you enormous headaches. Learning to live with a few little quirks of your workers is one of the requirements of being a manager.

Richard, a vital member of an engineering team, is late in turning in his report. His delay puts other members of the team behind schedule and this holds up the entire project. If, after constructive criticism, the behaviour continues, a reprimand is certainly in order.

Helen is required to keep a daily record of all transactions. It must be completed by closing time, but several times she has taken long lunch hours and been unable to finish. She has left at the end of the day with the work uncompleted. This puts the company at risk with the insurers. A criticism after the first offence is in order. If it happens again, a reprimand is then called for.

Serious offences are those which jeopardise other workers or the company, in other words those which have a bad effect on results. Repeated serious offences always call for a reprimand.

Get it in writing

It is important to understand that a reprimand can sometimes be the first step on the road to dismissal of an employee. As can be seen in *Task 14*, it is vital that a 'paper trail' be established. One of the worst things that can happen is to attempt to fire an employee, only to have that person say, 'You never told me I wasn't doing my job. You never gave me a chance to improve.' This can have serious implications.

If you reprimand someone and only the two of you are present, then it is only your word against his or hers that the reprimand actually took place. What carries more weight is if after a reprimand you write a memo and send a copy to the person, and put a copy of that memo in the worker's permanent file. Even better is to have the worker sign a copy of the memo indicating that they've seen it, and then put that in their file.

Some managers use the following rule of thumb (although it is certainly not foolproof). They give no written memos for a criticism or a first reprimand. Everything after that, however, is documented in writing.

The advantage of written documentation of a reprimand is that at some later date, if there is a dispute over whether or not a warning was given, the paper record will be essential if an eventual dismissal results in an industrial tribunal.

How to reprimand

The most important part of reprimanding is being sure the worker understands what is happening. Now that we've seen what reprimands are and when they should be used, let's see how that statement works.

In our experience a typical faulty reprimand goes something like this. Sandy, the manager, is upset with Gil's work performance. He has already constructively criticised Gil. The performance hasn't improved. Now it's time for the reprimand.

Sandy calls Gil into his office and asks him to sit down. Then the manager says, 'How's the wife and kids?'

Gil nods that they are fine.

Sandy, the manager, says, 'You like the work here? You've done good work for us in the past.'

Gil nods and smiles.

Sandy fidgets with his tie, then says, 'I've been watching your work recently.' He looks up to see if Gil is following. Gil nods that he is waiting.

Sandy continues. 'It's not bad, but I'm sure it'll improve.'

Gil nods indicating he's also sure.

Sandy says, 'Well, I'm certainly glad to hear that. You're one of our top employees. I'm sure you'll go far in the company.' He shakes Gil's hand.

Gil leaves the office feeling terrific. The boss just called him in to give him a compliment on his performance. He even feels good enough to take the rest of the day off.

Confrontation

The problem, of course, is that Sandy never really reprimanded Gil. Gil, in fact, never knew there had been a reprimand.

Why?

It's a problem of confrontation. Any time you have to tell someone something they don't want to hear, you are going to get 'bad vibrations' from them. They aren't going to be thrilled to learn that they might suffer if they don't change. That fact isn't going to make this one of their best days. You know, too, that some people react to bad news in disturbing ways. They might:

Yell
Argue
Cry
Plead
Faint
Become physically violent.

None of the above is something you want to experience and, fearing a confrontation, you may end up giving faulty reprimands. Too often the worker never knows he or she has been reprimanded.

Avoiding confrontation

While you can never be 100 per cent sure how a worker will take a reprimand, you should remember two things. First, as a manager, you must sometimes give reprimands. Second, if the reprimand is constructive (if it contains the three basic elements), a bad confrontation is much less likely to occur.

Remember, the three elements to a constructive reprimand are:

☐ Reprimand not the person, but the identifiable
problem part of the work.
☐ Show how to correct the problem and achieve future
success.
☐ Let the worker know there are undesirable consequences
for continued bad performance.

A bad reprimand is bad. But a faulty reprimand is like none
at all. Give constructive reprimands, but be sure the worker
fully understands he or she is being reprimanded.

Promotions and Bonuses

A bonus should be given only as a reward for superior performance. A promotion should be given only when a worker has outgrown his or her present responsibilities and is ready to take on new ones. That is the ideal. Actual practice, however, is often far different.

Bonuses

There are many different kinds of bonus. The most common is the regular year-end bonus offered by many companies. Some companies, however, offer bonuses for everything from recruiting new personnel to having top sales.

While we have no qualms about specialised bonuses, we feel the year-end bonus is probably the most misused in the country. To see why, we need to understand what the real purpose of a bonus is.

Specialised bonuses

Pete manages a production line and for the last six months he has exceeded his quota. It is through his diligent efforts that the increased production has come about. One way the company can recognise his achievement is through a bonus (cash, company stock, or a prize). This lets Pete know he's appreciated. It also spurs him – and other workers – on to greater achievements.

Sally sells more houses than anyone else in the office during the month of August. As a reward she receives a free week's vacation in Tenerife. This is a sales bonus. Often announced in advance, it encourages salespeople to work harder and it rewards the hardest worker. (Frequently there are second- and third-place prizes to console those who also achieved, but did not win.)

The purpose of these specialised bonuses is to encourage and reward achievement. When the bonus is for a specific accomplishment, it is almost always effective. In the above examples, increased production and higher sales were directly related to the bonus.

Year-end bonuses

Regular year-end bonuses are quite a different matter. Many companies, particularly large institutional ones, regularly reward workers at the end of the year with a bonus that can sometimes be as much as 10 per cent or more of the worker's annual salary. Typically, such bonuses are awarded across-the-board during good years. The company made money, the workers are the company, therefore the workers should be rewarded.

While the logic seems compelling, it is flawed. The company may have made money because of economic conditions totally unrelated to its workers' performance. A new and unexpected demand for the company's product may have been totally responsible for increased profits. Why, therefore, should the workers be rewarded?

The converse also may be true. A company may run into a few lean years. The workers (and managers) could be contributing outstanding achievements. Yet external factors such as unfavourable exchange rates or a recession could stifle demand. The company loses money, hence there are no year-end bonuses. Yet, shouldn't those workers who had extraordinary achievement be recognised with a reward?

The economics of business often make year-end bonuses either gratuitous or impossible to give. Both situations are bad in the workplace.

What does a worker think if he or she has slacked all year and still receives a bonus because the company in general did well? Is this worker encouraged to greater achievement or does the bonus do the opposite – encourage continued mediocrity?

Or what does a worker feel who has put forth great effort and has achieved all the goals and more that were outlined for him or her, and then does not receive an anticipated financial reward because the company in general is doing poorly?

Even more difficult, what about a worker who has fallen into a pattern of receiving bonuses every year? If a bonus has been given every year for the last three years, then on the fourth year it's expected. It's come to be thought of as a part of regular wages. If a bonus *isn't* paid, the worker is going to feel as if something due wasn't given. He or she is going to feel angry or insulted, and will probably end up taking those feelings out of the job.

Ultimately the problem with year-end bonuses is that they don't do what they are supposed to do. They don't act as rewards. Either they end up being undeserved windfalls or they produce hard feelings. There is often increased staff loss after they are awarded: employees planning a job change hang on for the bonus first.

We encourage you, as a manager, to reconsider your policy with regard to bonuses. We recommend instituting specific bonuses for recognised achievements. Timing should be considered more important than simply giving 'regular' bonuses. This may enormously improve the productivity of your workers and your company.

Promotions

Promotions are often given as rewards, sometimes in lieu of bonuses. Archie does well at his present job, so we'll reward him by moving him up.

The effect, of course, has often been described as the 'Peter Principle' (from the book of the same name by Laurence J Peters). Workers are rewarded with repeated promotions until they reach a level of incompetence. When they finally reach a job they can't handle, they remain there hurting the company, or they are embarrassingly shuffled to the side.

It is vital to understand that promotions should *never* be given as rewards. Only praise and bonuses should be given as rewards for good work.

Promotions should be given for two reasons:

1. A worker has outgrown his or her present job and is ready for new responsibilities.
2. A worker is not doing well at the present job, yet there is another at which he or she might succeed. (A transfer.)

The rule is simple. *Reward achievement with a bonus; promote to get greater achievement.*

Managing Pay Cuts and Demotions

Pay cuts and demotions are two very difficult areas for managers to handle. Nobody likes to cut a worker's pay. No one likes to hand out a demotion. Nevertheless, they are both things with which some managers must deal. Pay cuts and demotions come about for various reasons. Sometimes, much to the chagrin of the manager, the company simply must cut back and pay cuts and demotions are handed round rather than redundancies. We'll look into handling these shortly. In other cases, however, pay cuts and demotions are given as punishment for bad performance.

As punishment

Our feeling is that pay cuts or demotions used as punishment are counter-productive. Sidney is simply not doing his job. His manager decides to demote him one level with a corresponding cut in pay.

What was the manager's goal? Probably it was to get Sidney to perform better. Will the demotion result in increased performance? Unlikely. Sidney is sure to be angered, perhaps outraged, by what happened. In retaliation he will probably *decrease* his productivity.

If, as a manager, you are concerned that a person isn't performing as desired, don't think pay cuts or demotion. Instead look into the chapters in this book on encouraging, criticising, and reprimanding. Use the techniques described there to get your goals accomplished.

A worker demoted or given a pay cut for punishment is like a wounded animal. He or she just lingers around the company bleeding on others.

As a transfer

If the worker is not able to handle the work, consider transferring the person to another position. A transfer to a more suitable job, even one with a lesser title and lower pay, can frequently result in a turnaround in worker performance, as long as it's handled constructively.

Difference between punishment and transfer

A pay cut and demotion as punishment often leaves the worker doing essentially the same task, but with fewer responsibilities and less money. This frequently results in resentment.

A transfer, if handled constructively, puts the worker in a new position (albeit with less pay and perhaps fewer or different responsibilities). The new position, however, can be viewed as a 'second chance' or as a new opportunity. It may result in improved performance.

As a necessity

Sometimes we have no choice in demoting and reducing pay. The company may be enduring hard times. Sales and income are down. Survival is at stake, and the only way the company can survive as a whole is by cutting back salaries and demoting some workers. This is a trying situation, but one which sometimes can be managed surprisingly well. Many companies, particularly in recent years, have weathered such adverse conditions without losing personnel.

The key is the method by which the pay cuts and/or demotions are handled. If the worker is made to understand the problem and to feel that he or she is not being singled out, then cooperation can usually be expected. In fact, sometimes such cut-backs can result in increased enthusiasm and productivity from workers.

There are three rules to follow which usually produce good results from unavoidable pay cuts and/or demotions.

1. Communication

Be sure the workers understand what the problem is and that it's real. They must believe that belt-tightening is currently the *only* possible solution.

A good method of communicating this information is through informal meetings and round-table discussions. Such settings give the workers as well as the managers a voice. Typically, the managers present the problems. Then the workers are given full opportunity to express their grievances (which they will surely have). Finally, management says something like, 'Yes, you are right. It is a shame. But it's what we have to do.'

This is an invitation for the workers to offer alternatives, which they surely will. Patience is the order of the day here. Each alternative must be explored to demonstrate that it really won't work. Ultimately, if in fact it really is the case, everyone at the meeting will be forced to see that pay cuts and/or demotions are really necessary for survival.

2. Equality

Once the workers see the necessity for belt-tightening, it is helpful if they understand that everyone will suffer equally. It can't be that one worker takes a pay cut while another doesn't (or what's worse, gets a rise!). It is also helpful if cuts are across-the-board, taken not just by workers, but by management as well. This is a particularly useful argument when dealing with trade unions.

All must believe they are in the same lifeboat if necessary pay cuts and/or demotions are not to destroy a company. If even one manager or executive is seen as floating luxuriously in a yacht, *everyone* will scramble to get aboard and the lifeboat will be upset and sink.

3. Swiftness

If pay cuts and/or demotions are really needed, don't delay them. Once workers are convinced of the necessity, move forward at once. Any delay will certainly be taken as evidence that the belt-tightening really isn't necessary. After all, if the company can afford to wait, things can't really be as bad as reported.

Alternatives

Sometimes it may be possible to sweeten the blow of a forced pay cut or demotion. Workers, for example, could be offered company stock. Another alternative is to agree to bonuses once the company's health returns. The pay cuts/demotions can be made to appear as a trade off. Take less now, but get more later on.

Of course, these techniques have limited application. A worker can't take unsaleable stock to the grocery store, or bank future 'iffy' bonuses. Nevertheless, sometimes the offer itself is worth more than what is offered.

The Decision to Dismiss

There is nothing more difficult for most managers to do than dismiss a worker. Dismissal implies failure. It also often results in guilt on the part of the manager. Many think, 'What right have I to ruin this person's life by dismissing him?'

As troublesome as dismissal may be, it is nevertheless sometimes a necessity. In this chapter we'll look into the decision process involved. We'll also examine some of the steps you, as a manager, may want to take to ease the risks of dismissal and to make it more palatable.

Reasons for dismissal

It's important to understand that different reasons require different kinds of decision.

For example, a manager may have an excellent worker for whom he has nothing but praise and hope, but because of economic conditions he must dismiss the employee. Here the redundancy decision is made either directly by someone else or directly by economic necessity. Either way, it is a difficult task, but at least from a decision viewpoint, there is little room for the manager to manoeuvre.

At the other end of the spectrum, the employee may commit a gross misdemeanour which justifies the manager ordering instant dismissal.

In many cases, however, the situation is that a worker simply cannot function in his or her current job. The manager must decide whether to keep the worker on in the hopes of improvement, redeploy him, or – having gone through the necessary processes – terminate his engagement.

In some cases, the necessity for terminating employment

may be apparent to both the worker and the manager. There is no great confrontation and little emotional stress. The worker leaves on his or her own initiative and parts friends with the manager. This, as we'll see, is the ideal method.

Redundancy

Where redundancy or lay-off is involved, managers have a social duty to plan ahead to reduce its effect.

1. A workforce can be reduced by natural wastage, when workers who leave are not replaced, and the existing staff are redeployed.
2. The manager can call for voluntary redundancies, but the response is likely to be related to the package offered.
3. The operating procedures can be reappraised to reduce numbers and/or working hours to mitigate the effects of redundancy, even though this may call for cutbacks in freelance or casual workers, or in subcontract work. Job-sharing may be considered.

All companies which need to make workers redundant should have an established procedure.

If there is a recognised trade union in the company, the employer is legally obliged to consult with it in advance over the proposed redundancy of its workers.

Alternatives to dismissal

As part of the decision process it's important to consider whether there are alternatives. If you look carefully, you may find many in your own work situation.

Transfers

A transfer is the most common alternative to dismissal.

Patricia was hired to do accounting work. She was a bright, outgoing young woman who loved to talk to people. Unfortunately, this worked against her. Instead of focusing her mind on her books, she would chat with whoever came by her desk. Her warm friendly manner soon made her extremely popular with the other workers. Unfortunately, her work was dismal. It soon became apparent that Patricia was not going to be able to handle the accounting job. Her manager gave her objectives, encouraged, criticised, and even reprimanded her. She wanted to do the work, but her personality was just not suited to it.

Faced with firing this charming young woman, the manager actively sought an alternative. It turned out that there was an opening for a person to handle reception and invoicing work in another part of the company. The manager talked to Patricia about a transfer which meant a step-down in pay. However, Patricia knew she wasn't doing well and felt terrible about her current work. The transfer seemed like a second chance and she grabbed it. If things worked out, within six months she'd be making as much as she was as an accountant.

Patricia was a success at her new job. She was good at invoicing, with her accounting background, and she had plenty of opportunity to chat as a receptionist.

Change of responsibility or supervision

In this case an alternative that made sense all around was found. Other alternatives involve giving the problem worker more responsibility (or taking some away if the person has too much). So-called 'self-starters' need a free rein to achieve. Give them control over their work and they may blossom. Alternatively, a routine worker may need to have more supervision.

The point is that even within a particular job, transferring the direction of the work better to suit the temperament of the employee may be a realistic alternative to firing.

Moving to the side

It's important to distinguish between a realistic transfer, such as indicated above, and a sideways move. A transfer as a realistic alternative gives the employee a second chance in a more suitable job where he or she can succeed. A sideways move simply sends the worker to another job out of the manager's way where he or she isn't likely to get into trouble (or to succeed). This moves the worker into a 'non-job' where the person simply exists with little hope of achievement. It may motivate the employee to find a new job elsewhere. As the saying goes, 'When they want to get rid of you, first they put you in a smaller office then they take away your coat-stand.'

Moving a worker sideways usually occurs when a manager doesn't have the courage or the ability to dismiss outright and doesn't want to take the trouble to arrange a creative transfer. Joan wants to get rid of James, but she just can't bear the emotional confrontation of a dismissal. So instead she 'promotes' him into a useless job.

He has been pushed on one side. He may have little or no responsibilities and duties. There is no contribution he can make. He simply sits there, an embarrassment to both himself and the company. It's humiliating for James. Taking away the possibility of achievement robs him of all motivation and he gets depressed and becomes morose. Joan feels sorry for him, but because she doesn't have the heart to get rid of him, she lets him dangle there indefinitely.

Moving an employee to the side destroys morale all round and should be avoided. It is always better to try and dismiss outright and give the person a chance to succeed elsewhere than to have an empty shell hanging around the company.

Dismissal as a management failure

There's an old maxim that is frequently quoted in teaching: 'There are no student failures, there are only teacher failures.' Translated to the workplace it would read, 'There are no worker failures, there are only management failures.' Of course, there are times when things don't work out and it's not the manager's fault. A worker can have personal problems. A manager can inherit a bad worker. Or there may simply be irreconcilable personality differences between the worker and the manager.

But generally speaking, the manager has great opportunities to bring workers along. If the management job is done properly – beginning with recruiting satisfactorily – then there really shouldn't be many worker failures. You should be able to develop and build successful employees.

On the other hand, if it turns out that you're faced with dismissing many people, you should perhaps look at your own management performance. Perhaps there's something that you're doing wrong that needs to be corrected. Maybe your management technique is at fault. Perhaps the failure really isn't so much in the workers as it is in yourself.

The ideal in dismissal

Hennessey was an old and experienced manager. He had been with the company for over 15 years and had supervised hundreds of workers. Yet, though employees had come and gone, Hennessey had actually dismissed only a handful during the entire time. Mostly, the bad workers left of their own accord.

One day the managing director called Hennessey in and asked for his secret. 'You have a way with workers. How do you avoid dismissals?'

Hennessey sat back in his chair and put it as simply as he could. 'I don't need to fire people. When a worker sees that he can't do the job, he fires himself.'

The MD was intrigued. 'When they see they can't do the job? What do you mean? How do they see that?'

Hennessey seemed surprised by the MD's questions. 'It's quite simple. If Joyce is working for me, she knows what the job involves. We both clearly understand the performance required and the objectives. We both work towards her achieving success. If she can't succeed here for some reason that neither of us can control, then it's only natural for her to want to move to another place where she can. She knows that what I want most is her success.'

'Yes, I think I see,' said the MD. 'Only what if she's afraid of not being able to find other work? What if she's satisfied just hanging on even without success? Or what if she doesn't care that you know she's failing? Don't you have to take action then?'

Hennessey looked puzzled. 'Perhaps we're having a communication failure. When I said she knew I wanted her to succeed, I didn't mean to limit that to this job. True, I want her to know my own success at work will only come about through her work success. It's mainly because of this that she trusts me and works with me.

'But she also knows I want her to succeed, not only at this job at this time and place, but in her life as well. I want her to be a successful person.

'Once she understands that, that I'm really on her side, then it's very hard for her to stay on here in a mode of failure. If she's afraid about finding another job, I'll help her overcome her fear. I'll help her look for other work. If she's just hanging on repeatedly failing, then I'll know that she has some deeper problem and try to get her to seek outside advice. People don't normally seek failure, they seek success and achievement. As long as I keep that as the cornerstone of my relationship with her, I can't go far wrong.

'If she knows that her success is first in my mind, she has to care about what I think. I encourage her to achieve and she is motivated to do just that, if not at this company, then somewhere else.'

'Remarkable,' the managing director said. 'And it always works?'

'No, of course not. I'm far from perfect. I have my own problems and my own needs. Sometimes I really don't think about Joyce — about my workers first. Sometimes I make mistakes and fail as a manager. And sometimes I just can't establish rapport with a worker. In those cases I may have to fire.

'But I understand the ideal and work toward it.'

The 'ideal' which Hennessey sought is, of course, having workers who are so motivated to seek success that when it becomes apparent they aren't finding it at his company, they immediately move elsewhere. These workers aren't the type to slack through the day or to deliberately court dismissal and live on unemployment benefit for a few months.

Ideally, we hire workers who wanted to achieve. Ideally, we build on this motivation. If for some reason they don't achieve, then they should be sufficiently motivated to remove themselves from the current workplace and find another where they can achieve.

Of course, even as Hennessey understood, the ideal is something to aim at. We don't always achieve it. Even Hennessey, with all his experience, sometimes wasn't successful. On occasions even he had to fire his failures.

Making the dismissal decision

Except when a gross misdemeanour is involved, the decision comes down to two choices: can you keep this employee, work with him or her to improve their work or behaviour, *or* should you fire, appoint someone else, and start again?

There's an old maxim that goes, 'The devil we know is always preferable to the devil that we don't.'

We feel that if there is any way you can get involved with the worker to achieve improvement, then you should make the attempt. A bad worker transformed into a good worker is an enormous plus both to the company and to the manager. Nothing looks better on your record than to be able to take a liability and turn it into an asset.

On the other hand, it is important to be realistic:

☐ Is the worker unable to handle the job even with additional training?

☐ Does he or she not have the right temperament for the work?

☐ Is this the wrong person for the job?

If your answer to any of the above questions is 'yes', then you ought to seriously consider dismissal.

Dismissal Procedure and Documentation

Apart from causing emotional stress to both manager and worker, a badly handled dismissal can involve a company in confrontation with the trade union whose member is involved and/or a complaint by the aggrieved employee to an industrial tribunal. The stress mounts and work can be disrupted.

It becomes more difficult to dismiss an employee once the initial six months' period is over – hence the practice of some companies of employing workers for six months only. In some companies, in fact, passing the probationary period means the employee is virtually immune to firing except for severe cause. (Almost no one is immune to lay-off, of course.) Nevertheless, it is still possible to dismiss an employee for a good reason in most situations provided the proper procedure has been followed. In this chapter we're going to look at some of the procedures and documentation that may be needed.

Fair reason for dismissal

The 'fair' reasons for dismissal are normally one of the following:

1. Redundancy.
2. The employee's misconduct. If this is construed as a gross misdemeanour (eg dishonesty, damaging company property) peremptory dismissal may be the consequence.
3. Incapacity of employee to perform his or her job (going to prison for an offence unconnected with the job is *not* a 'fair' reason).
4. Inability of employee to continue in the job without breaking the law.

5. Repudiation of contract by the employee (by striking, for example) provided the employee is not singled out as an example.

Examples of unfair dismissal

1. The employer cannot provide a good reason for the dismissal.
2. The employer has not acted reasonably in the circumstances, ie he may have dismissed an employee without following the recognised procedures.
3. 'Constructive' dismissal, when the employee is placed in a position where the employer virtually forces him to resign.

Fairness has many interpretations. For example, a worker cannot be dismissed for taking time off work for jury service nor for engaging in trade union activities.

Similarly, a company cannot dismiss an individual who refuses to break the law. A manager wants to be sure that deliveries are made on time so he demands that his drivers get from one destination to another in so many hours. But doing so requires the workers to drive faster than the legal speed limit. A worker whose employment was terminated for refusing to meet the time requirements by breaking the speeding law would have a case for wrongful dismissal.

Probationary and permanent employees

Many companies write in a 'probationary' period which allows both worker and manager to see how things work out. If the worker is able to handle the job, then 'permanent' status is conferred after six months. If the worker is unable to perform as required, then it is understood that he or she may be dismissed.

It's possible for a company to get into trouble because it refers to its non-probationary employees as 'permanent' workers. The word 'permanent' of itself suggests that the job is guaranteed. Perhaps better words to use would be 'establishment' staff.

Problems in dismissing an established employee

Special problems arise when a manager tries to dismiss an established employee. These problems stem from the fact that once an employee has passed through the six months' probationary period, he or she has indirectly been given the company's stamp of approval. After six months have passed the fair reasons for dismissal listed on pages 99-100 apply.

Some managers really don't perceive what the difficulties are here. They feel that if the person isn't performing the job or if their behaviour isn't suitable, then he or she should go.

The law, however, requires that you consider not only the employee's immediate performance, but performance over the whole period of employment. It also requires that you consider any promises given and expectations aroused. Finally, it insists that you let the person know what the problem is and give them an opportunity to correct it.

For example, Sammy is not currently performing well. His manager, Hazel, has gone through the various tasks from encouragement through criticism to reprimand. She has explained what's wrong and given him a chance to correct it. But for the past six months, Sammy just hasn't done any work, so Hazel wants to fire him.

But Sammy has been with the company for 10 years. During that time he received regular pay increases and promotions. He has even received one or two commendations for his efforts on special projects. Written reports by his previous managers have been filled with praise. In addition, when the subject of termination is broached, Sammy protests that in the past he has been promised a 'job for as long as you want it'.

Finally, Sammy points to other workers who have been with the company who have had periods when they were having trouble and yet weren't fired. He knows one worker, Clive, who slacked for nearly two years without being discharged.

Hazel has her work cut out for her. If she attempts to fire, Sammy may come back with a wrongful dismissal claim. He can point to:

1. Good past performance with a record of positive reviews and even commendations.
2. Approval from the company in the form of pay

increases and promotions and a promise of employment virtually regardless of effort.

3. Company history of not dismissing others who had the same offence.

On the basis of Sammy's past 10 years, promises made, and expectations aroused, Hazel does not have much of a case, *unless* she can clearly document his current bad performance and demonstrate that dismissing him falls within set company and employment law procedures.

Absenteeism

Absenteeism, rowdiness, and inability to perform work can often be directly related to the consumption of alcohol or other drugs. If a worker's performance suffers or his co-workers have problems from behaviour arising from obvious or repeated drunkenness or overt drug abuse, then dismissal procedures could be invoked.

However, this may not be as easy as it seems. Alcoholism, for example, is today widely considered a disease. A worker cannot be dismissed merely because he has an illness, unless his state of health prevents him carrying out the job he was engaged to do. Therefore, drunkenness by itself may not be a sufficient cause. (In addition, the worker might claim that the work itself drove him or her to drink!) However, no company rules forbid alcohol on the premises or specifically bar employees who are the worse for liquor. These clauses could be invoked in a dismissal procedure.

To get rid of an habitually drunk employee, the manager may first make an attempt to correct the problem. A worker with a drug-related problem may need to be offered help, not forced into unemployment.

If the worker refuses offered rehabilitation and/or counselling or is repeatedly not helped by it *and* is unable to perform his or her job, dismissal may be the only solution.

Having a dismissal procedure

In order to dismiss effectively, it is advisable for the company to have a dismissal procedure. This consists of a series of steps that are to be taken before any employee is dismissed. This procedure is usually notified to managers in writing by the personnel department, and possibly made available to employees, sometimes in a company manual.

There are at least two advantages to having an established procedure. The first is that it clearly states the steps that must be taken. A manager thus knows what he or she must do in order to terminate a worker's employment. The worker, too, is also made aware of the steps. This means that if the steps are followed, the worker cannot claim that the eventual dismissal came without warning.

Additionally, a dismissal procedure avoids the claim that one worker was given preferential treatment over another. If the procedure is followed in *every* case, then a worker can't claim that a manager let a similar problem lapse with another employee.

A typical procedure

The actual procedure used by your company is important, but perhaps more so is simply having one that is used regularly.

The following is a typical firing procedure. It is not applicable in all cases but covers the legal requirements.

Step 1. Regular reviews, with the worker's problems clearly stated. Salary increases, bonuses, or promotions might be withheld on the basis of these reviews.

Step 2. Criticism

Step 3. Oral reprimand

Step 4. Written reprimand(s). The number of reprimands required may vary.

Step 5. Written warning(s) that the worker must correct problem or may be dismissed. (Number of warnings given may vary.)

Step 6. Investigation into the facts (which may be accompanied by the worker's *suspension* for a short period with pay). This could give the worker time to reconsider performance (unusual); or it may be for the purpose of investigating the worker's difficulties. If dismissal is decided upon, it is wise to check the case over before taking the irrevocable step in case an industrial tribunal is later involved.

Step 7. Written notice of job termination presented in person to the worker.

Notice that the procedure has a definite pattern, based on informing the worker each step of the way that there is a problem and what's involved in correcting it. Each step of the way the worker may improve performance and thus stop the procedure. The procedure is continued only if the worker's performance continues to be unacceptable. Each step should be noted on the employee's permanent file.

A good rule to remember with a dismissal procedure is that it should be *fair, informative and firm*. Additionally, the procedure should emphasise that *the problem is with performance, not with the person*.

Documentation

Documentation means creating and saving a written record. It involves following the steps of the procedure in writing. Documenting is a tiresome, troublesome job most people would prefer to avoid. Consequently, we tend to ask ourselves, 'Do I really need to bother recording this?'

The answer is *yes!*

Of course, if the worker does not enter a claim and no problems result, there really is no need for documentation. However, if there is a claim to an industrial tribunal, then virtually the *only* thing that can back up a dismissal is written documentation. Since you can never know in advance if there is or is not going to be a problem, the rule is to *always document every step*.

What to document

The answer is, record everything for every employee. Document everything because you never know what will turn out to be important later on. Three years after the dismissal, you can prune the file and only retain sufficient paperwork to provide a reference in case of need.

The following items are commonly documented:

Reprimands
Reviews
Warnings
Suspensions
Any disciplinary action
Notice of termination of employment.

What to include in documentation

On each document certain basic items should be included. Not including them may not be fatal, but their inclusion adds strength to the document.

Point

The document should state what it is. If it's a reprimand, then it should say so. If it's a warning, then that should be clearly stated. This avoids a worker coming back later on and saying that he or she was given a piece of paper, but didn't know what it meant. Putting the *point* of the document right in the heading is a good idea. In addition, you should state where in the overall procedure this document fits in.

Person, place, time, and date

The name of the worker, the job title, the name of the manager, and any other relevant information regarding the person should be included. The place the document was handed over as well as the time can also be included. In addition, the time of the problem (or the period during which it occurred) as well as where it occurred can be mentioned, as can other persons involved.

Problem

The document should clearly state what the problem is. If the worker is not performing duties, it should explain (A) what is expected; (B) how the worker is not performing; (C) how the lack of performance is affecting the company (such as lost sales, stockouts, etc).

Remediation

The worker must be given a chance to improve. The manager should explain the steps for improvement (if any) agreed upon with the worker and the time-scale for improvement. The document should clearly explain the consequences if performance does not improve. (If there was no agreement, the manager should explain why not and what further action is contemplated.)

Signature

This is perhaps the most vital part of the document. It's one thing to put a piece of paper in a worker's file. It's quite another thing, later on in front of a tribunal, to prove that the worker actually saw that document (or a copy of it). The problem is solved, of course, if the worker signs for the document. Then there can really be no doubts.

A worker should be asked to sign a copy of the document. That's the ideal. In the real world, however, workers may well refuse to sign such a statement.

If the issue is crucial, eg at board level, another director might be called in to witness that the document was handed over.

Time-scale

From what's been said thus far, you may get the impression that dismissal is a long, drawn-out procedure. Unfortunately, that may be true; a time has to be set within which the looked-for improvement must take place. What's usually involved is taking enough time to build up the necessary documentation.

Of course, for gross misconduct, dismissal can be immediate, and the employee has forfeited his rights.

Pitfalls to avoid

We've already suggested many of the pitfalls that a manager could get into, but there are some others that bear special attention.

Failure to supervise during probation

Managers tend to be rather busy people. There are lots of things to do and time is frequently very tight. Therefore, it's only natural to put off doing something which isn't urgent. One of those less-than-urgent items is to review the progress of a probationary employee.

Linda was taken on and at the end of each 30-day period her manager needs to review her performance, tell her how she's doing, and make recommendations for the future. Her manager, however, is very busy and puts off doing the review. Suddenly, the whole six months have elapsed. Linda's probationary period is ending. It's time to decide whether or not to keep her. Her manager looks at her performance. It's terrible. She hasn't done one thing right. In fact, she's made a nuisance of herself and hindered other workers. 'Get rid of her!' is the manager's decision. But Linda protests. 'It's unfair. No one told me I wasn't doing what was expected. No one said where I was going wrong. How was I to know? If I had been told, I would have done better.'

The manager didn't do her work. She didn't follow procedure and she doesn't have any documentation. Linda is entitled to her statutory period of notice, or payment in lieu.

Failure to discuss the problem with the worker

Sometimes managers will think that simply handing out written reprimands and warnings can be enough. That's usually not the case.

It is important that the manager attempt to explain the problem and find a means to a solution with the employee in good faith. Simply warning without making the attempt to find a solution is not enough. The worker might actually have a very good reason for not performing. For example, it would be embarrassing at the least to realise after dismissing someone that the worker was making mistakes because he had a serious but correctable eyesight problem that he was unaware of or was reluctant to have investigated.

Failure to allow sufficient notice

Although we've been emphasising this point throughout the chapter, it bears mentioning again. In today's world a manager does not simply walk up and fire a worker without notice, not if that manager wants to keep his or her own job.

Workers have rights and they are protected. To dismiss a worker, normally a case must be made. An important part of the case is providing sufficient notice so that the worker understands what the problem is and has the opportunity to correct it. If you spring dismissal on a worker, you could be in trouble.

Overlooking severance pay

Severance pay is frowned upon by many managers. Why should they give money to a person being dismissed for inadequacy?

One reason is that it may keep the person from coming back with a tribunal. It's not pleasant to think of it as a bribe, but if paying a small amount of money now can avoid paying a large amount of money later (not to mention headaches and time lost), then it may be a good investment.

Acting in anger

A worker does something wrong, something which really upsets you. You want to resolve the issue and get satisfaction right away. In short, you want revenge. So you storm out and fire the individual.

Except in cases of gross misconduct, dismissal should never be done on the spur of the moment. The consequences to you and the company could be serious. Take the time to clear your head. Make it your policy never to act until at least 24 hours have passed.

Then investigate. Be sure you really know what's happened. Be certain you have the right person and that they really did or didn't do what you think.

Then *follow procedure* and *document!*

It's the procedure and documentation which will protect *you* in the end.

Dismissal Interview

The hardest part of dismissal is undoubtedly the final interview itself. The real stress point comes when the manager informs the employee, often face-to-face, that the job is terminated.

In this chapter we'll see how to dismiss correctly. We'll also look into the emotional stress that often accompanies job termination.

Emotional stress on the manager's part

Managers often feel enormous guilt about dismissing. The manager may feel as though he or she is ruining the worker's life. A job is, after all, a livelihood. Dismissal takes away another person's means of earning a living. In a very real sense it could mean putting that person on to the street.

What if they can't find other employment? What if the dismissal is the final straw that turns them into a dropout? In the greatest extreme, what if next week's paper reports that they committed suicide — is the manager responsible?

Such can be the feelings of a manager who has to fire an employee. There's a germ of truth in these feelings, which is what makes them so compelling. But there is the other side of the picture that managers need to focus on.

Who's responsible

An employee is equal to yourself in every way except for the job position you hold. In other words, the employee is an equal human being — a person responsible for what happens in his or her life.

If you have followed a fixed procedure (as detailed in Task

14), then before dismissal you will have made every effort to inform the employee of the problem and to offer an opportunity to correct it. Ultimately, therefore, the reason you are dismissing is because the worker has chosen not to change, not to correct the problem.

To put it another way, if you have been fair in following your procedure (going from criticism to warnings), then it is the worker's actions which resulted in the termination. He or she knew that dismissal was a consequence (both from oral and written warnings), yet the worker chose not to take corrective steps. The worker, therefore, is the one who is ultimately responsible for the dismissal.

Accepting responsibility is what being a mature human being is all about. If you are to accept your responsibility as a manager, you must be willing to dismiss workers who don't perform. Similarly, workers must also be able to accept the consequences of their lack of performance.

Dismissal isn't the end of the world

A dismissed worker will most likely find another job. And the new job may be more suited to that person's skills, talents, and temperament. In other words, you may actually be doing someone a favour by dismissing that person from a job he or she can't handle. Remember, people are resilient. The worker will usually rebound and perhaps be better off for what happened in the long run.

When your job calls for you to dismiss, accept your responsibility and do it unflinchingly. Dismiss the worker, get it over with, then move on. Don't ever look over your shoulder and wonder.

Where redundancy is involved, the worker(s) should have had advance notice of their impending departure, and the company should do all possible to ease the situation for them in advance.

Emotional stress on the part of the dismissed employee

It's important to understand that, bad as you may feel when dismissing someone, the real emotional pain is on the part of the worker. Don't expect the worker to comfort you. Rather, you may need to comfort them.

Some dismissed employees have described their feelings at the time they were terminated as a little bit like being told they had a terminal illness. Much research has been done into the emotions involved with dying and it is generally accepted that there are at least four basic steps that people go through. People who are fired often experience the same phases:

1. *Surprise*. There is almost always surprise at the actual dismissal even if the person knew they were going to be dismissed.
2. *Argument*. The person may laugh, or show total disbelief to get you to say that it really isn't true, that it's a big joke. They may try to talk you out of it.
3. *Anger/Depression*. These are really two sides of the same thing. Anger comes first. The dismissed worker may suddenly blame you and even shout and rage. Then, sometimes very soon afterward, the person may redirect their anger at themselves. Self-directed anger, however, tends to be expressed as depression. They may slump down and sink into a depressed state.
4. *Acceptance*. Ultimately the dismissed worker will accept the dismissal and will move on to finding a new job.

The entire course of this four-stage emotional reaction typically takes several days. Some managers, however, have reported seeing many of the steps passed through in just the few minutes that it takes to handle a dismissal meeting.

When the worker experiences this emotional stress, it is important to understand there isn't a lot you can do. Comforting is helpful. However, the worker may simply have to suffer an emotional upheaval until he or she accepts the dismissal. If you recognise that what's happening is relatively normal, you shouldn't panic or otherwise be thrown off-balance by it.

The time of dismissal

Probably more than half of all workers whose employment is terminated are dismissed late on Friday afternoon. There's a good reason for this.

A dismissal should be a clean break. There is nothing worse

111

than dismissing someone and then having them hang around the office for a few days or weeks. That person becomes the living dead. Other workers don't know what to say to the dismissed employee. You can't really give the person orders because he or she doesn't work for you any more. To have a dismissed person remain on the job for a period of time is embarrassing and potentially damaging to the morale and productivity of the remaining workers.

Some managers are concerned about having dismissed employees work off termination or severance pay. Don't consider it. Dismissed employees will give you 10 per cent of their attention, if that. As soon as they are dismissed, their full-time job becomes finding other employment, not finishing up work for you, except in a redundancy situation.

All of which is to say that, ideally, a dismissal will be a clean break. The employee is terminated, picks up his or her final cheque, clears out the desk or work station, and permanently leaves.

The reason that Friday afternoon is most often selected is because it is the end of the week and the dismissed worker would normally have the next two days off. These two days are an excellent cooling-off period. During that time the dismissed worker can transition through the emotional steps of the dismissal. A worker dismissed on a Friday afternoon is least likely to provoke a scene or to show up the next work day to badger the rest of the staff.

A worker dismissed at 4.45 can usually clear out his or her desk and finish up after the other workers have gone home. Again it avoids embarrassing situations.

Some managers are concerned about the increased shock to the worker of getting dismissed right before the weekend. True, this can be emotionally trying for the worker who may have anticipated a calm weekend. But dismissal is going to be shocking at any time. At least on Friday night the shock is entirely the dismissed worker's and isn't spread among the remainder of the workforce.

The written dismissal

The worker should be given a written dismissal notice. It should state clearly the name of the person, the name of the company, the name of the job and, most important, that the person has been terminated. Some notices go on to indicate the reason for termination, and if the worker has been employed over six months, he or she has a right to a written statement of the reasons for termination.

The importance of the written notice is that it adds to the documentation. With written notice, the worker can't claim that he or she misunderstood. It's there to see in black and white.

Dismissal notices also have their dark side. Some managers use the dismissal notice as the vehicle for dismissing the worker – the 'pink slip' with Friday's pay packet. Dismissing a worker by using *only* a written notice is wrong ethically, practically, and economically. From an ethical viewpoint, the worker is entitled to be told, face to face. It's only common decency to do so.

From a practical perspective, getting only a written dismissal notice may be confusing. The worker may have some practical questions to ask. The manager has gone home and there's no one to give answers. So the worker shows up next Monday and an embarrassing meeting ensues. Rather than avoiding confrontation, the technique may actually provoke an even more difficult confrontation.

Finally, getting only a written dismissal notice would be likely to anger the worker to the point of retaliating against the company. A tribunal, even if won by the company, can be a time-consuming and expensive experience. From an economic viewpoint, it's usually far better to give the worker a few minutes of personal time.

The dismissal meeting

The dismissal meeting is when you tell the worker that he or she is fired and may hand them the dismissal notice and, usually, a final pay cheque. There is no way in which this is not going to be a difficult meeting for both of you, but it need not last long. And it can provide the worker the opportunity to make a final statement.

It can be a positive meeting for you. It can clue you up on whether or not the worker plans to pursue a wrongful dismissal claim. You can also sometimes gain valuable insights into your own management techniques. Workers may say things at the dismissal meeting that they were afraid of saying before. You may come to realise things you are doing badly that you never before saw.

Some managers come to dismissal meetings with a number of items to cushion the blow. Besides the last pay cheque, the manager may be in a position to discuss severance pay. (Sometimes it is advantageous to get the worker to agree here on a specific amount of severance pay.) Or the manager may be able to offer a temporary continuance of benefits (frequently an important item to dismissed workers).

The meeting itself

There are seven good rules that a manager should keep in mind when going into a dismissal meeting. These should help keep things on the right track.

1. *Don't have a dismissal meeting when you're angry.* Be sure you're calm and can think clearly.
2. *Don't keep the point of the meeting a secret.* As soon as the worker comes in, tell the person that he or she is dismissed. Yes, you can shake hands and exchange a 'Hello, how are you'. Then state the reason for the meeting. Any delay shows weakness and indecision on your part.
3. *Don't discuss the person.* You're not a therapist. It's not your position to tell people what's wrong with them or what they need to do to improve. They could be outraged if you try to.
4. *Do sympathise, don't apologise.* You can sincerely say you're sorry that things didn't work out. You can empathise and say that you can understand how difficult this must be for them. But don't apologise. Apologies make the worker think that you are in some way to blame. Apologies make it sound as though it's your fault that the person was dismissed. It's not your fault. At this stage of the game, finding fault is pointless. You are doing your job and you have nothing to apologise for.
5. *Don't rehash the problem.* The point of the meeting is to tell the worker he or she is *dismissed*. It is *not* to go over your firing decision. If you rehash the worker's problem, you can open a Pandora's box of whining,

promising to improve in the future, and cajoling as the worker tries to get you to reconsider the dismissal. Your mind is made up and nothing will change it. The decision is final.

6. *When things get tough, talk about the future.* The worker does have a future beyond the confines of your direction and your company. Point that out and try to get the worker future-directed. This dismissal may actually turn out to be a good thing for the worker, if it moves him or her in a positive direction. Many workers who knew the current job wasn't working out will admit this, and may themselves turn the meeting into a positive event. Looking forward will help both you and the worker to get past the present moment.

7. *Listen carefully.* Besides emotional stress, is the worker giving clues about taking possible retaliatory action? What kind? Is there anything you can do or say now that will head it off? Also, is the worker saying something valuable about your management technique? Are you paying attention so that you can improve yourself?

A typical dismissal meeting takes about 10 minutes. If you see that it's taking longer, simply end it. There really isn't a whole lot to say, and dragging things out can get messy for everyone concerned.

After the meeting

After the dismissal meeting it's a good idea to write up a brief statement of what happened. This is part of the documentation and should be placed in the worker's permanent file.

Managerial Faults to Avoid

We all want good employees. They make the company strong and they reflect favourably on us. Getting employees to work hard and do a good job, however, can be tough. Even when we pay them high salaries many seem to have their minds on something else or to be downright uncooperative.

Sound familiar? It's the lament of most managers. While there are usually a few self-starters around that work hard and produce, many workers often seem to be lackadaisical.

Wouldn't it be a wonderful world if *all* employees brought energy and enthusiasm to their work? That would make your job as a manager sweet and simple, wouldn't it? It would leave you with time to get your own work done. And it would go a long way toward making *you* look like a top manager in the eyes of your own boss.

This section will examine a strategy aimed at accomplishing just that. It's a plan which, if you adopt it starting right when you hire, could change your whole management style and produce surprising results.

1. Dealing with Lazy People

There are many reasons why people appear to be lazy. Pathological depression can cause it. Physical illness can give the same impression. Crushing personal problems such as divorce, death of a family member, or even a drinking problem can also take the vigour out of an individual.

All of these causes are really beyond your control as a manager and when you encounter them, you should suggest that the person involved seek counselling or get medical help. *It is always a mistake for a manager to try to become a therapist.*

On the other hand, a great many employees who don't have such personal problems also appear unmotivated. It's the behaviour of this group that you can attempt to change. But in order to make an effective change you must accurately understand why the person seems lazy. The answer to that question is something most managers don't like to hear. *Managers are usually the ones who drive employees to exhibit lazy behaviour.* (Sometimes it's the manager the employees worked for before you took over the department or before you appointed them.)

The manager's role in lazy behaviour

To see how managers produce lazy behaviour, let's get back to basics. Let's talk about natural human instincts.

Most people would agree that a natural human instinct is that of survival. Someone who doesn't want to survive, who has a death wish, is commonly considered to be mentally unbalanced.

We would suggest that another natural human instinct is

the desire for success. *All people want to succeed.* Just as a person who wants to die might be thought of as insane, a person who wants to fail, in our society, might likewise be considered 'crazy'.

The desire to succeed is as much a part of our natural instincts as survival. What happens is that along the way some people become convinced that they *can't* succeed. They begin to believe that the avenues to success are closed to them.

In a school a student gets a few bad exam results and suddenly loses the teacher's praise. The student tries even harder but, having fallen behind, gets more bad results. Now the student sees that even with hard work, the results are poor, and begins to believe that the ability to succeed in school (or a particular subject in school) is beyond reach. The avenue to success has been closed. 'When I work hard I do badly, when I don't work hard I do badly. Why bother to work hard?'

To observers, the student appears lazy. In reality, the student has simply lost the motivation to succeed. If this starts in second or third year, imagine what kind of a poor student we'll have in secondary school. And in college we've 'suddenly' got a lazy teenager.

The lazy employee

In the workplace it's not much different. An employee who fails at a few tasks forfeits the praise and rewards that come from successful work. Efforts may be redoubled but now it's particularly hard because there may be catching up to do. In addition, other employees may begin thinking of this person as cackhanded. The employee may fail at a few more tasks and come to the conclusion that even if he works hard, he isn't going to be a success in the workplace, won't get praise from the boss, won't win monetary rewards, may even be dismissed.

This employee will come to believe that the avenues to success in this particular workplace have been cut off. If he believes he is doomed to failure, he simply goes through the motions. To managers who are observing his behaviour, he is typically seen as lazy.

The manager as producer of lazy behaviour

The role of a manager is similar to that of a teacher in school. If a teacher creates situations where a student can succeed, the results, even for a 'lazy' teenager, can be astounding. (That's what's meant by the difference between ordinary teachers and good teachers.) In study after study where a 'poor' student is given opportunities for success, behaviour reverses itself. The student suddenly perks up, gets good marks, stops being 'lazy'.

If managers provide opportunities for employees to succeed, even workers who have long histories of 'laziness' will reverse their behaviour, turn around and become enthusiastic, energetic, and even dedicated once they see their avenue to success is open.

You may not wholly accept this concept yet, so we'll go into examples of how managers create bad employees to see how it works. First, let's deal with one other kind of worker.

2. Dealing with Uncooperative People

Next to the lazy worker, the most difficult employee to deal with is the one who is uncooperative, perhaps even belligerent. This employee may not actually take a swing at you, but he or she will purposely do many other things to make your life miserable, in addition to completing only the minimal amount of work required. When you assign a task he may take your instructions literally, hoping to fail and then be able to blame you for not clearly telling him what to do. He may exhibit behaviour you don't like, such as wasting time at the stationery store. As soon as you tell him to change that behaviour he substitutes another time-wasting activity, such as talking to another employee. 'You only said "Don't hang around the stationery store",' is his reply.

You know he understood what you meant, but he is deliberately baiting you, challenging your managerial skills.

Why employees are uncooperative

Uncooperative employees are usually smart ones who at some point realise that the avenues to success have been closed. But these people are smarter than the lazy workers who simply blame themselves; they are smart enough to know where to place the real blame. Managers have cut off the chances to succeed, so now these employees are going to make managers pay.

You may not have been the actual manager who originally cut off their chances to succeed. These people may be striking out at all managers. You just happen to be the first available target.

The remedy here is the same. Open up the road to success

and the uncooperative behaviour will be reversed. When the uncooperative employees see that success is attainable, they will go after it. Enthusiasm will replace uncooperative behaviour.

You still may not buy this concept, so now let's look at some real-life examples to see how managers cause the very behaviour they are trying to prevent in their workers. We'll also look at how providing opportunities for success reversed the undesired behaviour.

3. The Manager who Doesn't Delegate

Sally was managing editor of a national women's magazine. She had enormous responsibilities. She was responsible for finding writers, choosing stories to run, dummying the magazine, writing titles and subtitles, working with artists who designed the editorial material, and much more. And she had to do it all every month for each new issue. It was far too much for any one person to do. But Sally wasn't expected to do it all. She had a staff of seven editors working for her.

Sally's real job wasn't editing, it was managing. She had enough staff, but they were lazy workers. They wouldn't do their jobs, so she ended up doing the jobs for them. All the associate editors were always standing around drinking coffee, while Sally was putting in 16-hour days and still not getting it all done. She had a lot of staff turnover and last year she fired the whole bunch and brought in new people, but these were no better than their predecessors.

She'd say, 'I've asked my staff to come up with suggested titles for articles in an issue. In a few minutes they'd have them. But, invariably, they were awful. The staff are just too lazy to sit down and spend the time it takes to come up with good titles.'

Or she'd say, 'I'd ask an associate editor to find a contributor for a story. He'd give me three names. He'd be too lazy to follow through. So I'd have to interview each contributor and then make the assignment. My people are simply too lazy to follow up. That's why so many quit or get fired.'

Eventually someone suggested to the publisher that maybe the problem wasn't the editors, maybe it was Sally. The publisher considered this seriously and suddenly Sally's own job was in jeopardy. She had to remedy the situation quickly, but how?

124

'I just can't find good editors,' Sally said, and threw up her hands in despair.

Maybe. But William Randolph Hearst, who built the famous Hearst empire of newspapers and magazines, was reported to be able to take almost anyone who just happened to be walking along the street, bring them in, and in a short time turn them into a good editor. If he could do it, why couldn't Sally?

Asking the obvious

We asked Sally why didn't she consider letting her people take the blame for their work? Why didn't she tell the associate editors that this month the titles they came up with would be used. She'd only veto outrageously bad ones: otherwise the associates' titles would definitely go into the magazine, no matter what. If they were bad, the associates would have the blame.

Sally laughed. 'Isn't that wonderful sounding. Let them take the blame. But I'm the one who'll really take the flak from the publisher, not them. If there are bad titles, it's my neck.'

Next we suggested that Sally tell an associate to find a writer for a story, do the interviews, make the assignments, and come up with the article. Whatever he came up with would be used. She would veto it if it was truly terrible; otherwise, it would run.

Sally chuckled. 'Sure, and if it's a hopeless article? We still have to pay for it and I have to account for the money to the publisher. And if we run a crummy article, the magazine suffers and it's my neck again. My people are simply too undependable to take a chance on.'

We asked Sally how she could be so sure. She replied that it was obvious, they had never done the work yet. We asked if she had ever really given them the responsibility. Had she ever really delegated the authority to any of her associate editors?

Delegating success

Sally didn't know the measure of her employees because she

had never really given them responsibilities. Maybe some of them were indeed poor editors, but maybe some were good ones. We asked her to consider it from the associates' viewpoint.

Her subordinate editors were never given a whole job to do. *They were always given only part of a job*. They always knew that Sally would take over the responsibility at crucial junctures. They knew that no matter what they did, Sally would finish it. No matter how hard they tried to contribute, Sally would see to it that their work would never appear in the magazine.

What did that tell them? It told them that there was no way for them to succeed. Sally did all the work, took all the responsibilities, and left them with menial tasks. Thus, their jobs became unimportant. They moped around appearing 'lazy'. (Actually, they were just waiting for other, better jobs to open up.)

Coping with fear

'Why would I do that?' asked Sally. 'I want good strong employees.'

The answer was that she was afraid of failing. Sally felt herself under the gun from the publisher. She had to come up with quality each month. She was afraid that if somebody else's work wasn't adequate, she would get the blame. So she constantly fell back on doing things herself until there was so much to do that she was overwhelmed.

We showed her that she needed to realise that the problem was her own fear and that she had to face it.

Facing it for Sally meant really delegating work to others. The first month she told her staff that they would create the titles for articles and whatever they came up with would be used. It nearly killed Sally to watch the editors struggling with titles. But it also impressed her. They worked late, had meetings, consulted with one another, and finally came up with a list.

Right away, Sally knew their titles weren't as good as the ones she could have created. She wanted to chuck them all and write new ones herself. She could have done it in a few hours. But the titles weren't all that bad, either. The magazine probably could survive one month with them. So, as part of the experiment, she gritted her teeth and agreed to use them.

The result was astonishing. Suddenly the formerly lazy employees came to life. They had actually successfully completed a task. They saw their titles in print. They immediately began planning titles and stories for the next issue. They began going out to find contributors. They demanded more responsibilities.

Fearfully, Sally let out the reins. Suddenly she found she was leaving at five o'clock while some of her staff were working late. The publisher noted the change right away and nodded approvingly toward her. Of course, it was all superficial. The real test would come with the next issue.

Sally couldn't sleep the night before the staff submitted the titles and the articles. She had worked with them, helping when asked, but it was their work. Now she'd have to accept what they did because it was too late to do it all herself. The staff submitted their work. Sally carefully looked it over and had to admit most of it wasn't bad. In fact, some of it was quite good.

Sally never did overcome her fear completely. She still did too much of the work herself. But at least she knew she had a problem. Now when an editor started to act 'lazy', she would ask herself whether she was causing the problem. She would say to the editor, 'I've got a challenging assignment for you.' Holding her breath, she would delegate the authority that gave the other person a chance to succeed.

4. The Manager who Doesn't Give Necessary Information

Peter was the general manager for a well-known chain of restaurants. It was his job to see that over 90 different locations were well run and up to the company's standards. To do this, he was responsible for the regional supervisors and the individual managers at each location. While Peter delegated some personnel responsibilities to regional supervisors, he nevertheless toured the country stopping at each location to evaluate the local managers and staff.

Everywhere Peter went he found sloppiness. The managers simply weren't keeping the restaurants up to company standards. In some cases the staff wouldn't all be wearing regulation uniforms, or weren't friendly enough to customers. In other situations meals weren't prepared exactly as they were shown in the colour pictures on the menus. Sometimes carpets weren't clean or silverware and plates weren't fully dried before being placed in service. It was laziness pure and simple. The managers just weren't taking the time to be careful. Peter pointed out the problems, dismissed some managers, and appointed others. He changed the regional supervisors. When he went back, things were no better. Staff turnover in the restaurants was high, compounding the problems. The managers seemed unresponsive to his demands. No matter what he said or did, it seemed things only got worse. 'Managers are the laziest people in the world,' was his favourite expression.

Peter felt he had the toughest job in the company. It was up to him to keep up the standards of the whole restaurant chain. He redoubled his efforts and saw to it that the company president knew how much effort he was putting out. As bad as things were, he knew they could be far worse, would be far worse if it weren't for him. 'Why, I'm indispensable,' he would point out every chance he got. 'Without me there isn't a chance this company could survive.'

Peter was on the road 10 months out of the year. At a typical stop, he would enter the restaurant pretending to be a customer, sit down and order a meal. He would check the performance of the waiters and waitresses, the quality of the food, and the cleanliness. He'd keep an eye out for how busy the place was in order to check receipts later for signs that the manager might be skimming the profits.

Always there were problems. After his meal he'd track down the manager and talk with him about whatever he perceived the problems to be and say he expected them to be corrected. When he returned a few months later, the original problems might be solved, but invariably new ones would have cropped up.

On his return visits, he'd get angry and bawl out the manager. Usually the person would look guilty and promise to do better. This continued for nearly a year until one day a manager angrily said, 'If you don't know what you want, how the hell do you expect *me* to know!' The man left on the spot. Peter thought about that for some time and finally decided the man was neurotic. He wanted the restaurants clean, with good food, and good services. That should have been apparent to anyone.

A few weeks after that incident, Peter was called to the home office. He expected a promotion or at least a bonus for his outstanding work. Instead, he was *dismissed*.

In a state of shock, he asked the company chairman what the trouble was. The chairman told Peter, 'You never gave your people enough information. You never clearly spelled out exactly *all* your goals for them. You'd just pop up and say they were doing this or that wrong. They'd correct that, but they really didn't know what to do to get everything right. They've been living in fear of your sudden appearances and what, to them, were your arbitrary criticisms.'

'But everyone knows how a restaurant should be run,' Peter countered.

'In general, that may be true,' the chairman agreed. 'But when it comes to specifics, you have to make it perfectly clear what's expected and you have to listen to your people to see that they understand. We've had complaints about you for months from managers all over the country. Finally, one came in and told me what the real trouble was. I had to do something. The only reason we kept you on this long was because I felt you'd surely see the problem yourself and correct it.'

Why information is held back

Peter didn't give his managers what they needed in order to succeed because that way he felt he was indispensable, was more successful himself. In his greed for his own success, he kept it from his subordinates. Each time he saw a subordinate fail, it convinced him of his own value. In the short run, his success was amplified by the contrasts with the local managers' failures.

But in the long run, people (such as the head of the restaurant chain) are interested in results. On the one hand, it was obvious to everyone that Peter was a vital employee, touring the country and propping up local managers. On the other hand, it was just as obvious that the whole company was in trouble, suffering from poor management. The local managers, faced with no chance to succeed under Peter, had become lazy and sloppy. They weren't enthusiastic or even, in some cases, loyal. And it showed to the customers who responded by not coming back. Ultimately, the chairman realised that business was being adversely affected and he dismissed Peter. (Of course, if the chairman had never carefully explained his *own* goals to Peter it could be argued he was equally to blame.)

Some managers are so greedy for success that they try to build it on the failure of their subordinates. Sometimes unconsciously, they withhold the information necessary for the subordinates to succeed and when their workers fail they say, 'I told you so'. In the short run such a manager may look good by contrast, but in the long run when results are weighed, that manager comes out a loser.

5. The Manager who Refuses to Train

There is a short corollary here that is worth mentioning. Not long ago we came across Rosalind, a manager in the invoicing department of a large corporation. This manager had the habit of taking on employees with a bit of accounting background and then throwing them into credit control, simply telling them that their job was to get payments in. When an employee asked, 'What's company policy? How do we get someone who's three months late to pay up?', Rosalind would answer, 'Work it out for yourself. No one trained me, so why should I waste my time training you?'

Every few months there was a crisis. Accounts were too long overdue and the executives would come storming down to see what the matter was. Rosalind would simply smile and say, 'It's the new people. Inexperienced. I'll take over and see that it gets done.' She would step in, and in a week or so everything would get caught up. Rosalind was sure that the executives noted how valuable she was. As for the employees, they had learned their true value to Rosalind and felt angry that they weren't shown how to do the job properly.

When we last saw her, Rosalind was still doing the same thing. But executives in higher management were beginning to say that something had to be done about that manager in invoicing who was screwing up the works.

6. The Manager who Criticises all the Time

Joan was in charge of a production line at a large high-tech plant in California. She was responsible for over 30 assembly workers who hand-soldered integrated circuit boards to power supplies. It was painstaking work that required both dexterity and concentration.

Joan watched the assembly line like a hawk. She would move up and down and whenever she spotted a problem, she'd pounce on the worker. 'That's a cold weld,' she would say. 'It'll work when we test the unit, but it'll come apart when it's bounced around in shipping and it won't work for the customer. Don't you know how much a returned product costs this company? It costs about two months of your salary. How would you like it if you were docked two months' salary? I bet you wouldn't. So don't let it happen again. You can be sure I'll be watching.'

Joan regularly bawled workers out in front of their colleagues. She knew she wouldn't win any awards for popularity, but she took pride in the knowledge that she ran a tight ship and that she was respected.

From the workers' perspective

The workers didn't respect Joan at all; they hated her. They saw it as a no-win situation. 'If I do good work, she never says a word. But let me make one mistake and she jumps on me.' If there was no way they could win, the workers were going to be sure that Joan didn't win either. As if by agreement, they all worked more slowly. When Joan was nearby, they were very careful to do accurate work. But the minute her back was turned (after all, she couldn't watch all 30 of them every minute), they'd sneak in a cold weld or crimp a wire so it would break after shipment, or do something equally destructive.

The ultimate result

Joan's workers became not only lazy, but uncooperative. It eventually showed up with the number of returned units. It didn't take long for upper management to realise that a lot of them were coming back because of shoddy workmanship on Joan's assembly line. It also didn't take much observation to realise that Joan's line was moving too slowly. Joan was hauled in and criticised by her superiors. She thought this most undeserved since she was working hard. But then she was shown the reason: poor workmanship and slow performance.

In a rage she flew down to her assembly line and on the spot fired five of her workers. She yelled at the rest and laid down the law in no uncertain terms. But production grew even slower and shoddy workmanship increased. No matter how much Joan increased her vigilance and criticised her crew, things only grew worse. Eventually top management came to the conclusion that maybe the answer was to dump Joan.

Before that happened, however, we spoke to Joan. We asked her, 'Why don't you stop criticising your crew?'

She scowled back and said, 'Look at the work they do. They deserve to be criticised.'

'Perhaps,' we replied. 'But criticising hasn't worked. Why don't you try a different approach? When they make a mistake, why not simply pull them aside, out of earshot of their fellow workers, show them what the problem is, and tell them how important it is to be careful. You might also try a few incentive rewards for those who do good work.'

Joan only shook her head. She continued her old ways and in a month she was fired. The manager who took her place, however, did listen, and that production line is now far faster and more accurate.

7. The Manager who Doesn't Praise

There is a short corollary to Joan's story, that of the manager who, while not criticising, also fails to praise enough.

Larry was in charge of a group of engineers who had the responsibility of coming up with improvements to his company's line of computer accessories. Larry's engineers were continually coming to him with new ideas. He always listened. He told some to proceed and others to forget it and try a different direction. Occasionally an engineer would come up with something that really worked. Larry would grunt, send the person back to work and forward the item to marketing or elsewhere for evaluation.

When the employee would stammer, 'But don't you think it's a terrific idea?', Larry might reply, 'You're getting paid to come up with terrific ideas. You want a pat on the back, too?'

Larry explained that they all knew the work was a departmental effort. They all knew that good products would eventually make all of them look good. They were all adults here and nobody was so childish as to need perpetual encouragement.

The employee's viewpoint

The engineers saw it differently. When they brought creativity, energy, and enthusiasm to their work, they wanted to be recognised for it. Larry's grunt and refusal to pat them on the back both figuratively and literally made them feel that they actually didn't have an accomplishment. It diminished their work and took away their feeling of success.

After turning in a good project, more than one engineer

had commented that they didn't feel they wanted to work for the company any more. One thing they all seemed sure of. After one or two experiences with Larry, they sure weren't going to bust their guts for the company in the future. Many became listless and simply hung to their jobs while keeping their eyes open for opportunities elsewhere.

Results are what count

By withholding deserved praise, Larry was actually turning their success into failure. In the process he was undermining his whole department.

As we've said, people are ultimately concerned with results. Eventually Larry's department came in for criticism from higher management. It just wasn't producing as it should. This reflected badly on Larry. Now he had a choice to make. To get production up he was going to either have to start praising more — something he considered childish — or he was going to have to give his workers that other surefire reward, more money.

(One manager we know uses this rule of thumb: 'For each time I fail to praise a higher-level employee for a job well done, I have to add money to his or her year-end bonus. If I don't, they'll quit or become lackadaisical on the job.')

A few words of praise are certainly cheaper than thousands of pounds in bonus payments.

8. The Manager who Takes all the Credit

Our last example may be the worst type of manager of all: the one who takes credit for other people's work.

Teddy was data processing manager of an aerospace firm. He worked with hundreds of programmers, engineers, and marketing people and was indirectly responsible for developing programs and processing techniques to aid the company in the creation of a series of components that would ultimately come together in a new weapons system for the Air Force. Much of the work involved breaking new ground, creating new technology; Teddy's department was responsible for coming up with new and innovative computer programs.

Teddy felt that he was on the firing line. Besides keeping the regular data processing going, he had to be constantly coming up with new ideas to satisfy the company's project directors. At his level, management positions were relatively scarce and competition was awesome. Either he produced or they'd get someone else who did.

To get the most from his workers, Teddy would take his employees aside and tell them, 'This is a good company and it's expanding. The way for you to get ahead is to hitch yourself to someone who's moving up. I'm aiming for a job as a major project director, eventually a company director. Maybe some day the presidency. Do good work for me and when I move up, I'll remember you.'

It was a pretty effective little speech and it usually had the desired results on his workers, at least at first. They were enthusiastic, creative and energetic and the results were some remarkable programming innovations. Teddy would heap praise on them and tell them they would go far. The employees would leave feeling terrific, feeling successful.

Then Teddy would take the product to one of the directors

and say, 'Here's a new idea I came up with in my spare time.' If it was a good idea, the director would heap praise on Teddy and tell him how wonderful it was for the company that he was working there. Teddy would smile at all the points he was scoring.

The truth will out

Eventually the employee who actually produced the new program would one way or another find out that it was being used and that Teddy had taken credit for it. Perhaps the employee would see it in use and point at it in pride only to be told, 'Teddy came up with that.' Or maybe the employee would ask when his new idea would be used only to be told it was Teddy's idea and was already in use.

Whatever the way, once the truth was known it was a blow to the employee. In some cases the worker would simply stop producing for Teddy. He'd become sluggish on the job and Teddy would have to consider dismissing him. In other cases there would be an angry confrontation. The worker would storm into Teddy's office demanding to know why credit had been stolen.

Teddy had a story all ready. He would immediately admit that what the employee said was true. Then he'd say, 'So what? As I told you before, I'm on the way up. This just helps boost me faster. It doesn't matter that the directors don't know it was your idea. You and I both know it. When I move up, I'll remember and you'll move up, too.'

The employee's reaction

Most people know baloney when they hear it. There probably never was an employee who was entirely fooled by what Teddy said. Some may not have been quite sure, but most realised that if and when Teddy ever did move up, he'd be forced to get rid of them. After all, they knew something which could tarnish Teddy's reputation. They were, after all, a threat to him. Even after his little speech, those employees who didn't slow down (become lazy) began looking for new jobs.

137

The turnover in Teddy's department became heavy. This slowed data processing down considerably. Nevertheless, with his fancy stories Teddy was able to keep things going for a while. Eventually, however, *everybody* who worked for Teddy realised what was going on. Old employees would tell new ones and the production of new ideas in Teddy's department came to a halt.

Eventually Teddy was called to account. One of the directors asked pointedly, 'For a fellow who's always come with so many bright ideas himself in the past, why do you even need workers? Or were those always your ideas?'

Why managers steal the credit

Teddy's problem was that he was occupied with two negative emotions: fear and greed. On the one hand, Teddy was afraid to give credit for anything to another person. He was afraid that person might be recognised as superior and be advanced over him. Teddy was so insecure about his own capabilities that he saw all his workers as potential competitors. In other words, he *feared* them. On the other hand, Teddy was so driven to succeed that he became greedy. He began to think that by taking other people's success for his own, his own star would rise faster and higher.

He was wrong on both counts and the result for him was disaster.

9. Why Managers Lose

People are concerned with results. Thus managers who:

- [ ] Don't delegate authority
- [ ] Don't give necessary information
- [ ] Don't train their workers
- [ ] Criticise too much
- [ ] Praise too little
- [ ] Take credit for the work of others

are managers who ultimately fail. To put it another way, managers who don't let their subordinates succeed are invariably sowing the seeds of their own future ruin.

But is this always the case? After all, this can be a harsh and cruel world. Are we saying that the bad guy always loses and the good guy always wins? Can't there be a bad guy with all the bad qualities mentioned above who still gets productions up and is a terrific success as a manager?

We don't think so. It's possible in the short run, but not in the long run. As Lincoln is quoted as saying, 'You can fool some of the people all of the time, and all of the people some of the time. But you can't fool all of the people all of the time.'

The manager who doesn't allow his subordinates to succeed is doomed because the essence of managing is motivating people. And the single biggest motivator is the opportunity to succeed. Take that away and people simply won't perform. All of the above practices are self-defeating. They motivate people to cut back on results. That has to reflect on the manager and ultimately result in his or her downfall.

A winning strategy

Thus far we've presented our strategy negatively. Now let's look at it from the positive side. *The only way for you to succeed as a manager is to work your hardest to see that your people succeed.*

Remember, the desire to succeed is natural. We all want to succeed, and that includes everyone who works for us. The common thread running through all the examples we've given is that the manager in every case withdrew the opportunity for his or her workers to succeed. Reversing that, providing success opportunities, taps into that great desire your workers have.

Go out of your way to provide opportunities for your workers to achieve. Even the 'laziest' workers, the most 'uncooperative' workers, will suddenly perk up when they see that they are achieving things. And the more they are able to achieve, the better workers they will become. It's the old snowball effect. One small success leads to another. A series of small successes leads to bigger achievements. More and bigger achievements and you are building a successful worker.

You may not be able to change your workers' personalities or their abilities. But you can change their behaviour. You can inspire them to exhibit energy and enthusiasm on the job.

Will your workers' success reflect on you?

This is a big worry for many managers, particularly if they're the least bit like Teddy in our last example. 'Will it really directly help *me* if my subordinates succeed? Won't I just be creating powerful competitors?'

It's important to understand that our overall strategy isn't altruistic, it's selfish. We don't help others out of generosity. We do it out of self-interest. Enlightened companies spend fortunes to provide good working conditions for their employees including recreational facilities, study grants, and bonuses for extra effort. They aren't being generous. They know that doing these things will result in greater productivity. (Being 'enlightened' in business means, in fact, knowing where your self-interest really lies.)

When your workers succeed, the overall production of

your unit increases. Who gets the praise for that? When one of your workers comes up with a good idea, who remembers the manager who developed that worker? People (including bosses) notice what's going on.

A person who's really good is going to move forward either with your help or in spite of you. If Karen is a talented person who later achieves even greater success, are you going to be remembered as the manager who brought Karen along or as the manager who tried to stand in her way?

The strategy for building successful employees, therefore, is simply to do everything in your power to give your employees opportunities to succed. It may sound simplistic, but it *works!*

The 15 tasks already described have shown you what to do to ensure the success of those who work for you and thereby ensure your own success. But remember, the guiding light of your strategy should be this maxim:

The greatest motivating force in the world is the desire to succeed. Show a person how he or she can succeed and they will do anything for you.

Conclusion

If you've read through this book, you may find yourself drawing an unforeseen conclusion: it may seem that if you use common sense you'll come out all right.

Yes, common sense, in fact, is the key to dealing with most management situations. That doesn't mean, however, that you should run blindly into each problem trusting to your good judgement to bail you out. It may be that lack of experience, emotional upset (such as being fearful, hostile, or angry), or not fully appreciating the totality of the problem, could finish you. Rather, a cautious approach is suggested.

When you have a problem in management, use the following strategy. You may find it works even when common sense is nowhere to be found:

Stop!

Take a break. Leave the room or the building. Go for a walk. Take the time to cool down and gain perspective. Look at the big picture and see where the 'small' problem of the moment fits in.

Define the problem

What *exactly* is wrong? No, it's not that you have a 'lazy' worker. It's not that you have an unsurmountable difficulty. Cut your problem down to size. Is it the need to 'criticise' a worker? Should you give a 'reprimand'? Are you in need of 'documentation'? Is knowing what to ask in the 'interview' the trouble? Put a name to that problem and you'll be able to handle it.

Treat it as a task

Once you have the problem defined, think of it as simply a task to be completed. As a first step, refer to the tasks in this book. They offer 15 sound solutions to the most common problems in managing people.

The task approach

We call this the 'task approach' to management. We have found it works as an effective strategy in every management situation we've run into. We sincerely hope you will find that it also works for you!

Index